Read,

Write,

Inquire

Read,
Write,
Inquire

Disciplinary Literacy in Grades 6-12

Hiller A. Spires
Shea N. Kerkhoff
Casey Medlock Paul

TEACHERS COLLEGE PRESS
TEACHERS COLLEGE | COLUMBIA UNIVERSITY
NEW YORK AND LONDON

Published by Teachers College Press, 1234 Amsterdam Avenue, New York, NY 10027

Cover design by Patricia Palao.
Cover illustration by maxkrasnov / iStock by Getty Images.

Library of Congress Cataloging-in-Publication Data

Names: Spires, Hiller, 1956- author. | Kerkhoff, Shea K., author. | Paul, Casey
    Medlock, author.
Title: Read, write, inquire : disciplinary literacy in grades 6-12 / Hiller A. Spires,
    Shea K. Kerkhoff, Casey Medlock Paul.
Description: New York, NY : Teachers College Press, [2020] | Includes
    bibliographical references and index.
Identifiers: LCCN 2019032251 (print) | LCCN 2019032252 (ebook) |
    ISBN 9780807763346 (hardcover) | ISBN 9780807763339 (paperback) |
    ISBN 9780807778227 (ebook)
Subjects: LCSH: Language arts (Middle school) | Language arts (Secondary) |
    Project method in teaching. | Literacy—Study and teaching (Middle school) |
    Literacy—Study and teaching (Secondary)
Classification: LCC LB1631 .S665 2020 (print) | LCC LB1631 (ebook) | DDC
    373.236—dc23
LC record available at https://lccn.loc.gov/2019032251
LC ebook record available at https://lccn.loc.gov/2019032252

ISBN 978-0-8077-6333-9 (paper)
ISBN 978-0-8077-6334-6 (hardcover)
ISBN 978-0-8077-7822-7 (ebook)

Printed on acid-free paper
Manufactured in the United States of America

This book is dedicated to our first teachers—our mothers:

Margie Ann Joyner Spires,
Mary Ann Kerkhoff,
and Eva Medlock.

Contents

Acknowledgments

We have been inspired by the many teachers who have crossed our paths. Without them, it would not be possible to write a book on disciplinary literacy and inquiry. We would like to thank Emily Spangler from Teachers College Press, who initially sparked our interest in writing this book and has encouraged and guided us along the way. Thank you for understanding and appreciating the nuances of our approach to disciplinary literacy and inquiry.

Additionally, thank you to Rita Lewis, who provided outstanding editorial assistance. We appreciate your expert attention to detail and encouraging us to stay on schedule. Finally, Marie Himes, Jessica Eagle, Erin Lyjak, Andrea Gambino, and Sharon Wright—your input and support were invaluable in making the book a reality.

Introduction

Why do I have to eat vegetables? How do leaves change colors? How does a person learn to drive a car? Anyone who's been around children for a period of time knows that questioning and childhood go hand-in-hand, like hashtags and Twitter. As children progress into adolescence, their questioning progresses. Why was 16 chosen as the age for driving? What should the driving age be in our state?

The challenge isn't how to get students to ask questions; the challenge is how to harness their questions into deep content learning. Using disciplinary literacy as an approach to inquiry-based learning is an innovative yet sound way to connect students' interests and curiosities to the curriculum while simultaneously creating the conditions for deeper learning. In this book, we detail how the Project-Based Inquiry (PBI) Model can promote students' critical and creative thinking within the disciplines to answer real-world questions about topics that concern them.

Throughout our work with thousands of teachers in different contexts, we have observed their interest spark as they learn how to master the art of inquiry and apply disciplinary literacy approaches within the process. They are so drawn to the model and the scaffolds for each phase of the process as they integrate literacy strategies within their discipline that we believe the explicit phases of the inquiry process within the model set our approach apart from other work in disciplinary literacy.

DISCIPLINARY LITERACY AND PROJECT-BASED INQUIRY (PBI)

We define *disciplinary literacy* as reading, writing, speaking, listening, and viewing for deep learning and knowledge creation within a discipline. Our definition builds on the important disciplinary literacy work that has come before (e.g., Lee & Sprately, 2010; McConachie & Petrosky, 2010; Moje, 2015; Shanahan & Shanahan, 2008). The specific contribution we make focuses on knowledge creation as part of disciplinary literacy, which connects with our emphasis on student inquiry.

We relate disciplinary literacy to inquiry through our PBI Model (Spires, Kerkhoff, & Graham, 2016; Spires, Kerkhoff, Graham, & Lee, 2014), which is derived from the new literacies work of Don Leu and colleagues (Leu, Kinzer, Coiro, & Cammack, 2004; Leu, Kinzer, Coiro, Castek, & Henry, 2013) and ideas from project-based learning (Buck Institute, n.d.; Kingston, 2018). The five phases include:

1. Students compose a compelling question. The question can be generated by the teacher or the student, or through a collaboration between teacher and student. Students can work in pairs or small groups to explore their questions.
2. Students gather and analyze sources that relate to their question. They use a wealth of digital and print resources to gather pertinent information. We differentiate how experts in four core disciplines (ELA, science, history, and mathematics) might gather and analyze sources, and how they might conduct themselves during all phases of inquiry.
3. Students creatively synthesize claims and evidence that they generate based on the information they have gathered. For example, a literary critic might construct claims with textual evidence and close examination of language, and a scientist might construct models to support scientific hypotheses.
4. Students critically evaluate and revise their supporting evidence as they fine-tune their claims within a discipline. For example, a historian might detect inconsistencies in evidence and revise for strength and credibility of claims, while a mathematician might critically question logic and revise for precision.
5. Students communicate their products (that is, share, publish, and act) to a larger, global audience. Far too often, teachers are the only ones who see students' inquiry products. Students can produce inquiry products for a variety of audiences both inside and outside the classroom. Using social media to connect with audiences from other countries and cultures makes the experience much more exciting and allows students to share what they have learned.

HOW OUR MODEL IS DIFFERENT FROM OTHER METHODS

By relating disciplinary literacy to PBI with intentionality, teachers are able to guide students to learn the content of the disciplines and the processes that experts undertake to create knowledge. Thus, students have opportunities to construct new knowledge by employing the content knowledge and disciplinary literacy practices used by literary critics, scientists, historians, and mathematicians. From our experience with this model, making the intuitive practices of the disciplines explicit within an inquiry process opens up a rich context for deeper learning among teachers and students.

We acknowledge that disciplinary literacy is not a new idea. For decades, scholars at the college level have been interested in how reading and writing in one discipline—say, physics—is different from reading and writing in another discipline, such as history. Inquiry, likewise, is not a new approach to education. We could attribute the idea of inquiry-based learning to John Dewey (1927), the father of modern education. And deeper learning may be older still, with arguments about breadth versus depth of learning going back to ancient Greece. Although none of the concepts by themselves are brand-new, when combined in novel ways, they serve to energize teaching practices. Combining inquiry and disciplinary literacy is an idea whose time has come.

BENEFITS FOR TEACHERS AND STUDENTS

The Common Core State Standards and the state and national standards reforms that followed have set in motion a wave of energy around teaching *how* to think, not just *what* to think. Disciplinary literacy focuses on the reading, writing, and thinking processes that disciplinary experts use to construct new knowledge in a given field. Inquiry learning focuses on students' construction of knowledge through an inquiry process. By teaching students the process of knowledge construction, teachers show students *how* to think both critically and creatively. During the inquiry process, students think critically as they break down problems and evaluate sources, and then students think creatively when they synthesize multiple sources to create solutions to problems.

For example, as students work as scientists to investigate GMOs in their favorite corn chips, work as historians to interview their grandparents to understand life before the Internet, or work as literary critics to review the latest dystopian young adult novel, they plunge headfirst into the content of a discipline. It may not always be a graceful dive, but with each iteration their process becomes smoother and smoother and their learning goes deeper and deeper. Throughout the book, we look at the subject areas of English language arts (ELA), science, history/social studies, and mathematics to illustrate differing processes for learning in the disciplines. Our hope is that eventually, students will be able to use their deep disciplinary knowledge to inquire about the interdisciplinary problems in the world.

CHAPTER SUMMARIES

Our first chapter, "Disciplinary Literacy and Inquiry for Deeper Learning," lays the foundation for what disciplinary literacy is and why it is important for deep learning. The chapter explains the difference between content-area reading and disciplinary literacy—the difference between general literacy skills that can be used in any context and the specific ways of reading, writing, and thinking that scientists, historians, mathematicians, literary critics, and other experts use to create ideas. Though both are important, disciplinary literacy promotes deeper learning in a content area because it describes the social practices and cognitive processes that experts use within a discipline.

Chapter 2, "Relating Disciplinary Literacy to Inquiry Through the Project-Based Inquiry (PBI) Model," explains how inquiry is related to disciplinary literacy, and how combining the two can lead to deeper learning for students as they investigate research questions that spark deep curiosity. We introduce our model for relating disciplinary literacy and inquiry for deeper learning, called Project-Based Inquiry (PBI). In PBI, students ask a compelling question; gather and analyze sources; creatively synthesize claims and evidence; critically evaluate and revise; and share, publish, and act.

In Chapter 3, "Gathering and Analyzing Sources: Getting Close to Close Reading," we explain how to gather and analyze sources for credibility and accuracy, and how to conduct close readings in the disciplines. During close reading, a reader analyzes a complex text for meaning and evaluates the conclusions an author makes. Students also use close reading to consider the author's craft and think about the decisions that writers make when communicating to an audience. Craft choices are dependent on audience, and more important, dependent upon discipline. Students read closely to learn how writing in history is different from writing in science. In this way, students close-read to learn to write in the disciplines.

Chapter 4, "Creatively Synthesizing Information: Building Digital and Global Literacies," illustrates how students can synthesize claims and evidence in service of their compelling question as well as represent this information in creative ways. The chapter takes readers on a tour of digital tools that integrate technology with reading, writing, speaking, listening, viewing, and visual representation. We also demonstrate how to use PBI in a global instructional context. During PBI Global, teachers break down the walls of their classrooms to explore and take action on global issues represented by the United Nations Sustainable Development Goals. We share how schools have collaborated on globally relevant inquiry projects with schools and external experts around the world, such as civil engineers, children's book authors, and community activists.

In Chapter 5, "Critical Evaluation as Summative and Formative Assessment," we describe how to differentiate the inquiry process to meet students' needs and take advantage of students' interests so that all students engage in deeper content learning. We also discuss formative assessment of disciplinary literacy as students are apprenticed in the disciplines and summative assessment as students assume responsibility for their learning.

Chapter 6, "Share, Publish, and Act: Students and Teachers Stepping into Leadership," invites teachers to support their students to share and act on the work they create and to become experts on disciplinary literacy and inquiry in their content areas for their community. The chapter lays out a professional development plan that readers—principals, literacy coaches, or teachers—could implement in their schools.

DESIGN FEATURES

We use several design features to engage the reader. First, we insert questions that ask the reader to *reflect* throughout each chapter to support the reader in active engagement with the disciplinary literacy and inquiry concepts and practices that are introduced. Second, at the end of each chapter, we have a brief summary of the chapter ideas and a section titled "Now It's Your Turn!" that guides readers through planning and conducting a PBI within their class. Finally, the appendices contain sample lesson plans for inquiry-based disciplinary literacy for ELA, science, history/social studies, and mathematics, as well as a template that can be used with any disciplinary or interdisciplinary topic. The lessons are also available online:

- *English/Language Arts*—tinyurl.com/PBIDLELA
- *Science*—tinyurl.com/PBIDLScience
- *History/Social Studies*—tinyurl.com/PBIDLhistory
- *Mathematics*—tinyurl.com/PBIDLmath
- *Template*—tinyurl.com/DLPBItemplate.

Get ready to dive into disciplinary literacy and inquiry!

CHAPTER 1

Disciplinary Literacy and Inquiry for Deeper Learning

You don't want to cover a subject; you want to uncover it.

—Eleanor Duckworth

Education is not the learning of facts, but the training of the mind to think.

—Albert Einstein

Diving into disciplinary literacy and inquiry necessitates thinking about two ideas separately as well as together; to successfully engage students with deeper learning, educators must understand the fundamental aspects of both disciplinary literacy *and* inquiry. In this chapter, we provide foundational ideas about disciplinary literacy and inquiry before introducing the Project-Based Inquiry (PBI) Model delineated by discipline in Chapter 2.

WHAT IS DISCIPLINARY LITERACY?

As an emerging concept in the literacy field, disciplinary literacy is becoming better known through the implementation of new frameworks and standards that emphasize the concept, such as the Next Generation Science Standards, the 3C Framework for Social Studies, the Common Core State Standards, and new state standards. These standards require students to think critically about complex texts. A shift is occurring from content literacy—reading, writing, and speaking standards tied to the study of literature in English class, for example—to disciplinary literacy, or reading, writing, and speaking tied to using evidence from informational texts in English, history/social studies, science, mathematics, and other technical subjects (Lee & Sprately, 2010).

With the shift in the standards comes a shift in instruction. Teachers in all subjects are wondering: What exactly is disciplinary literacy and how am I supposed to teach it? Disciplinary literacy involves advanced literacy skills and disciplinary ways of thinking: reading, writing, speaking, listening, and viewing for deep learning and knowledge creation within a discipline. We agree with Lent and Voigt (2019), who claim that "because disciplinary literacy honors the expertise of teachers and asks for their participation instead of their compliance," it encourages their "willingness to try new practices and set higher standards and goals for their students" (p. 21). Students need to learn these advanced skills and dispositions within each discipline over time, which means that teachers across subject areas and across grade levels are responsible for teaching their students disciplinary literacy.

Literacy as a Social Practice

We view literacy through a sociocultural lens. Sociocultural theory places the learner in the center of sociocultural activities and suggests that interaction with others is essential to cognitive development (Hatano & Wertsch, 2001). As a social practice, this means that literacy is more than a finite set of skills to be acquired at one time. Instead, literacy is what people do with reading and writing for specific purposes, is influenced by different contexts, and continues to grow throughout our lives.

Rather than an isolated activity, literacy is about communicating with others; it takes place in three contexts: social, cultural, and historical. Social context implies that literacy is happening between people rather than independently. Individuals practicing literacy form groups, such as disciplines. Cultural context means that literacy norms differ between different cultural groups; each group has different ideas about what counts as literacy or which literacy practices are most helpful. And historical context means that what is happening today has roots in what has happened in the past.

As depicted in Figure 1.1, within context there is an interaction among the reader, the text, the author, and the task. During the reading process, readers activate their cognition, motivation, knowledge, and experiences (Snow, 2002). These attributes vary from reader to reader, making the reading experience unique for every person. The reader encounters a variety of challenges in the text depending on text complexity, which includes "surface code (the exact wording of the text), the text base (idea units representing the meaning of the text), and the mental models (the way in which information is processed for meaning) that are embedded in the text" (Snow, 2002, p. xv).

The author typically has a purpose for writing a particular text, and his/her background and intent are part of the text. (It's worth noting that Louise Rosenblatt [1978], however, argues in her transactional view of reading that the author is not part of the "meaning transaction" between the reader and the text; the author produces a text, but once it is finished, it must stand on its own.) If you are reading like a literary critic, knowing background information about the author as well as the author's purpose at the time of the writing of the text may contribute to the reader's understanding.

Figure 1.1. Literacy as a Social Practice Surrounded by Context

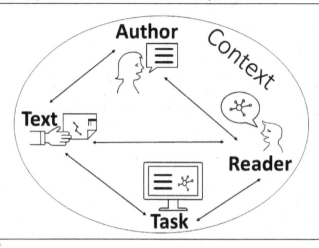

The reading task that confronts the reader may arise from an external force, such as a teacher making a reading assignment. Or the task may be self-imposed. In any event, the reader creates a purpose for reading, which interacts with other facets of the reading process. It's important to note that a reader's purpose for reading may change within any reading event.

Disciplinary Literacy as a Social Practice

We view disciplinary literacy with a sociocultural lens as well. This involves an apprenticeship model for learning: Those who identify as a disciplinarian help the newcomers to the group learn what literacy practices are the most effective and most valued for the purposes of the work done in that discipline. A historian does very different work from, say, a biologist, a physicist, or a poet. Because of that, the epistemological (or the knowledge creation) work that they do is different.

You can see how knowledge is created in mathematics in the popular movie *Hidden Figures*. The main character uses a mathematical method, Euler's method, to solve a new problem. Although this is fictionalized and the actual math used for the NASA moon landing project was more complicated, the movie illustrates how knowledge is constructed in mathematics. If Euler's method gives the right answer, then the mathematics works. This is different from literature, where there is no right or wrong method to creating a literary work. In science, knowledge is created through hypothesis-testing and laboratory research. And in history, knowledge is created through the gathering of original sources, such as photographs, letters, and newspaper articles. Experts use literacy in different ways—it's those specialized aspects of literacy that we're talking about when we discuss disciplinary literacy.

Discourse in Disciplinary Literacy

We know that disciplines include norms and expectations around discourse, which refers to the specialized language of a community. Restaurant discourse, for example, includes technical language like *sauté*, *julienne*, and *tenderloin*. Restaurant discourse also includes jargon like *86* and *FOH*. Shouting "86 turkey burgers!" means there aren't any turkey burgers, so don't let guests order any, but it's much quicker during a busy shift to say "86 turkey burgers." FOH stands for "Front of House," which refers to the host, servers, and general manager. In addition to vocabulary, social norms are part of language in a restaurant community. If you watch the Food Network, you may notice that contestants on cooking competition shows always say, "Yes, chef" when speaking to someone with a chef's credentials. When you talk to a chef, you are expected to be respectful and obedient and to refer to the person as *chef*; this is part of restaurant discourse.

As students learn to negotiate different discourse communities within the schooling process, it's extremely helpful if teachers make those practices and expectations explicit. It's not just about the content of English, history, science, and mathematics, but also about the discourse and how knowledge is constructed within the field. Emerging research shows that if students have access to knowledge about discourse and how knowledge is constructed within a field, deeper learning can take place.

Reflect: What makes up the discourse of your discipline?

The Disciplinary Mindset

Teachers of English, mathematics, science, and history/social studies are all dedicated to supporting students in gaining a deep understanding of the work done in those disciplines. The objectives are not merely to remember facts, but to be able to deeply appreciate a literary work or articulate how a problem was solved and why. One way to go beyond the surface domain of knowledge is to dig deeply into texts with a disciplinary mindset.

When we read a history textbook, for example, we are reading someone else's description of what happened during a certain event. We might learn who were the important people, what were the important places, and when the event happened. We take away what might appear to be facts, but historians look at events not as a set of facts but as claims that make an argument. A historian makes an argument of what he or she believes happened during a certain event using the most credible evidence he or she finds. Historians contextualize sources to determine when, where, and why sources were created. Think about reading the same text, but reading with the lens that it isn't a set of facts to be memorized but instead is a series of arguments.

History now requires critical and creative thinking! Instead of a bunch of information, the text becomes a series of decisions, an argument that someone created. The historian investigated by reading original sources and interpreting them. Students come to understand the role of context in history and tensions involved in the discipline. They realize that if the author had different documents, he or she might have written a different account. Most importantly, students achieve deeper content learning. A deep level of disciplinary understanding can only come when we engage with texts in the same way that the authors who wrote the text did.

Understanding that disciplinary literacy is a way in to deeper understanding within a discipline is important for teachers. It is also important for teachers to understand the difference between disciplinary literacy and content literacy.

WHAT IS THE DIFFERENCE BETWEEN DISCIPLINARY LITERACY AND CONTENT LITERACY?

As schools implement new state and national literacy standards across disciplines, disciplinary literacy is often equated with the time-honored practice of content literacy. Our first author, Hiller Spires, has taught content literacy for more than 20 years, and has witnessed the high impact that both strategies can have on students' capacity to process and comprehend text, especially for low- and average-ability readers.

There is a difference, however, between disciplinary literacy and content literacy in terms of how literacy instruction plays out in the classroom. Content literacy is associated with intermediate literacy (Shanahan & Shanahan, 2008), where teachers focus on comprehension strategies for a variety of texts as well as for studying and retaining information. Disciplinary literacy, however, is associated with advanced reading and writing, and is particularized to a specific discipline. It's important to understand the unique structures, practices, texts, and discourse of disciplines, as well as how knowledge is created and communicated in those disciplines.

Whereas content literacy is literacy *in* a domain, disciplinary literacy is considered the literacy *of* the domain (Ehren, Murza, & Malani, 2012). Content literacy may be seen as the tools superimposed upon a text to aid students' reading and writing skills, but Zygouris-Coe (2012) proposes that disciplinary literacy comprises core skills that are intrinsically tied to texts' unique structures and the "habits of mind associated with each discipline" (p. 42). Though content literacy and disciplinary literacy practices can be complementary, discipline-specific practices serve the unique purpose of stimulating deeper-level learning.

Complementary Practices

The view that reading skills develop hierarchically, as Jean Chall (1996) put forth, asserts that students progress developmentally from learning to read (basic literacy) to reading to learn (intermediate literacy) to using reading and writing to construct new knowledge (disciplinary literacy). By the time students reach secondary school, language in the content areas becomes more technical and abstract. Students are expected to be able to read, write, think, and speak in the different disciplines, which requires them to understand the nuances that exist in the different subject areas and to have strong foundational language skills (Ehren et al., 2012) as well as procedural knowledge of inquiry in the disciplines (Buehl, 2017; Moje, 2015).

However, the hierarchical progression of disciplinary literacy may be problematic. We have long been warned to resist a false dichotomy between learning to read and reading to learn. Even when students are learning to read, they can still be reading to learn. For example, Marcus, a 4-year-old, is reading sight words. He loves Mo Willem's book *I Love Slop!,* where a pig introduces the food of her culture, slop, to her elephant friend, who thinks it's disgusting. While Marcus is reading along and saying the words he knows aloud, he stops to ask his mother, "What is culture?" We know Marcus understands the explanation when he asks a friend from China visiting on Thanksgiving to describe the food in her culture. He is able to simultaneously learn to read and read to learn. Similarly, we never stop learning new words, so even as adults who are reading this book to learn, we may learn to read and understand a new word (like *epistemological!*).

In the same way that we should resist a false dichotomy between early (learning to read) and intermediate (reading to learn) literacy, Brozo, Moorman, Meyer, and Steward (2013) argue that we need to resist a false dichotomy between content-area and disciplinary literacy practices. In resisting the complete separation and "reconciling the divide" (Cervetti, 2014), we view content literacy and disciplinary literacy as complementary practices (Faggella-Luby, Graner, Deschler, & Drew, 2012). To bridge content reading with disciplinary literacy, some researchers have proposed discipline-specific strategies to aid students in constructing knowledge.

Discipline-Specific Strategies

English experts, for example, may analyze literature through a specific literary theory lens. Teachers can have students read a book with a critical lens using Lewison, Flint, and Van Sluys's (2002) four goals of critical literacy. In circles of four, each student chooses a "literary" role: disruptor of the commonplace, interrogator of multiple viewpoints, investigator on sociopolitical issues, and promoter of social justice through action. Our students used these roles to discuss Jacqueline Woodson's *Brown Girl Dreaming* and were able to collaboratively construct deeper-level questions and meanings from the text than a nondisciplinary reading for pleasure would have evoked (Lewison, Leland, & Harste, 2000). Disciplinary literacy strategies "encourage questioning, challenging, and understanding in ways that go beyond superficial content knowledge" (Lent & Voigt, 2019, p. 37).

Fang and Schleppegrell (2010) propose functional language analysis (FLA), which requires students to deconstruct how language is used differently across the disciplines. Teachers in social studies can teach the commonly used morphemes in social studies (*anti-, counter-, inter-, non-, trans-, uni-*); teachers in science can teach common science morphemes (*bio-, endo-, hydro-, micro-, photo-, therm-*); and math teachers can instruct students on common math morphemes (*bi-, centri-, deca-, equi-, multi-, poly-, quad-*). FLA gives students the tools necessary for close reading so they can construct meaning from the text and also create language to describe and explain the new knowledge that they create.

Another strategy that asks students to consider the disciplinary nature of a text is *inside-out reading*. Understanding complex vocabulary words, being aware of the author and context, and reading closely for meaning are a few of the literacy skills necessary in disciplinary reading, because this kind of reading is dictated by the text and moves from the inside out (Brozo et al., 2013). In inside-out reading, the content-area text governs the goals and processes needed for reading. Ultimately, content determines the process of close reading (Herber, 1970). We'll talk more about close reading in Chapter 3.

Reflect:
How do you use content and disciplinary literacy strategies in your classroom?

APPRENTICESHIP IN DISCIPLINARY LITERACY

Now that we have defined *disciplinary literacy*, it's time to explain how to teach it to enable students to learn deeply in the content areas. One approach to teaching disciplinary literacy is through the apprenticeship model. From an apprenticeship perspective, learning happens and knowledge is constructed in a community of practice (Lave & Wenger, 1991). Participation in specific communities requires members to understand the various repertoires, routines, tools, vocabularies, and ideas that are unique to the community. However, apprenticeship in the literacy of any given discipline enables students to access knowledge in different disciplines (McConachie & Petrosky, 2010; Moje, 2007).

The goal is not to have students become experts in every discipline, but to become critical consumers of texts in every discipline. We believe that having explicit knowledge in a discipline helps students understand that knowledge is constructed. This understanding potentially positions students to be critical readers and ultimately empowered to construct knowledge for themselves. We agree with Elizabeth Moje's (2007) argument that not teaching disciplinary literacy can become a social justice issue.

McConachie and Petrosky (2010) describe the apprenticeship model of teaching disciplinary literacy as learning on the diagonal, in which students actively and simultaneously display growth in their disciplinary habits of thinking and their content-area knowledge. Explicit instruction following an apprenticeship model consists of a gradual release of responsibility from the expert to the student, as depicted in Figure 1.2. This classic model of learning theory by Russian psychologist Lev Vygotsky (1978) was described as the gradual release of responsibility model by Pearson and Gallagher in 1983. Although the process is not always linear, it may begin with expert modeling and scaffolding, and results in students being able to independently transfer the skill or practice to a new problem.

An essential aspect of scaffolding is the deliberate fostering of productive talk within classroom collaborations. Fisher and Frey (2013, 2017) point out, however, that collaborative learning is often omitted within classroom instruction. Collins, Brown, and Newman (1988) put forth six actions that take place during apprenticeship:

Modeling: Expert demonstrates the practice.
Coaching: Expert guides and gives feedback as students attempt the practice.
Scaffolding: Expert supports students so that students are successful at the practice.
Articulation: Students think through the practice through talking or writing.
Reflection: Students compare their own practice with that of an expert or peer.
Exploration: Students apply the practice to a new situation.

Figure 1.2. Releasing Responsibility on the Diagonal from Teachers to Students

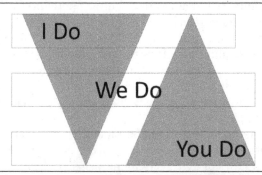

Adapted from Fisher, D., & Frey, N. (2013). *Better learning through structured teaching: A framework for the gradual release of responsibility* (2nd ed.). Alexandria, VA: ASCD.

Reflect:

What does the apprenticeship model of disciplinary literacy look like?

Disciplinary Literacy Progression in the Common Core State Standards

As students progress through the grade levels, their ability to negotiate complex disciplinary texts and tasks also progresses. Tables 1.1–1.4 show examples of how students may progress in their disciplinary literacy abilities based on the Common Core State Standards.

Table 1.1. Example of How Students Might Progress in English Language Arts (ELA) Literacy Based on the Common Core Standards

	6–8	9–10	11–12
Common Core State Standards	CCSS.ELA—LITERACY.RL.6.2 Determine a theme or central idea of a text and how it is conveyed through particular details; provide a summary of the text distinct from personal opinions or judgments.	CCSS.ELA—LITERACY.RL.9–10.2 Determine a theme or central idea of a text and analyze in detail its development over the course of the text, including how it emerges and is shaped and refined by specific details; provide an objective summary of the text.	CCSS.ELA—LITERACY.RL.11–12.2 Determine two or more themes or central ideas of a text and analyze their development over the course of the text, including how they interact and build on one another to produce a complex account; provide an objective summary of the text.
Examples from the classrooms	Working in small groups, write a paragraph that objectively summarizes the theme and create a digital presentation that gives textual evidence for a theme of a book the whole class read and discussed together.	Working independently, write a paragraph that objectively summarizes the theme and a paragraph that gives textual evidence for a theme of a novel the whole class read and discussed together.	Working independently, read a classic British novel of the students' choice and write a literary analysis explaining two or more themes.

Table 1.2. Example of How Students Might Progress in Science Literacy, Based on the Common Core Standards

	6–8	9–10	11–12
Common Core State Standards	CCSS.ELA—LITERACY. RST.6–8.6 Analyze the author's purpose in providing an explanation, describing a procedure, or discussing an experiment in a text.	CCSS.ELA—LITERACY. RST.9–10.6 Analyze the author's purpose in providing an explanation, describing a procedure, or discussing an experiment in a text, defining the question the author seeks to address.	CCSS.ELA—LITERACY. RST.11–12.6 Analyze the author's purpose in providing an explanation, describing a procedure, or discussing an experiment in a text, identifying important issues that remain unresolved.
Examples from the classrooms	Working as a whole class, students discuss the author's purpose for each section of a scientific text.	Working in small groups, students annotate a text to describe the purpose of each section of a scientific text. Students highlight the research question in the text.	Working independently, students read and annotate a scientific text, marking the author's purpose and any questions that remain unresolved. Students bring their questions to class for a whole-class discussion the next day.

Developing Disciplinary Identities

In the reading apprenticeship framework, Schoenbach, Greenleaf, and Murphy (2012) conceive of literacy through four overlapping dimensions: cognitive, social, personal, and knowledge-building. Through growth in each of these dimensions, students develop new disciplinary identities of themselves as learners. Rather than reading *like* a historian and writing *like* a scientist, students take on the identity of a historian and of a scientist.

These disciplinary identities "are enactments of self that reflect the habits of mind, practices, and discourses—of the ways of knowing, doing, thinking, and acting—associated with work in the disciplines" (Moje, Stockdill, Kim, & Kim, 2011, p. 8). By and large, building disciplinary knowledge and identity is an intertwined and interactive process during which learning occurs from constructing knowledge and navigating different contexts (Moje et al., 2011). Through apprenticeship in the literacy practices of a discipline, students are exposed to the methods employed within the field (Moje, 2015;

Rainey & Moje, 2012). Disciplinary insiders not only participate in practices similar to those of other members of that community, but they also identify with other members and the knowledge associated with the discipline. Thus, a disciplinary insider must be able to engage in the language, thinking, and social processes specific to the discipline (Fang & Coatoam, 2013). Yet, to apprentice learners toward mastery and participation as disciplinary insiders, there must be explicit instruction so that students can develop the skills of the discipline over time.

Table 1.3. Example of How Students Might Progress in History/Social Studies Literacy, Based on the Common Core Standards

	6–8	9–10	11–12
Common Core State Standards	CCSS.ELA—LITERACY.RH.6–8.9 Analyze the relationship between a primary and secondary source on the same topic.	CCSS.ELA—LITERACY.RH.9–10.9 Compare and contrast treatments of the same topic in several primary and secondary sources.	CCSS.ELA—LITERACY.RH.11–12.9 Integrate information from diverse sources, both primary and secondary, into a coherent understanding of an idea or event, noting discrepancies among sources.
Examples from the classrooms	Working as a whole class, make a Venn diagram showing the information that is present in both the primary and secondary sources that the class read and the information that is unique to each source. Students then work with a partner. One partner reads a primary source and one partner reads a secondary source. The partners then make a Venn diagram for their readings.	Using a jigsaw method, students read one of four primary or secondary sources on the same topic. Students then form groups of four, so that each student has read a different source. The students then write a paragraph that summarizes the information that was present in at least three of the sources.	Working independently, students conduct library research and interview primary sources on a chosen topic and write a research report of their findings, citing sources appropriately.

Table 1.4. Example of How Students Might Progress in Mathematics Literacy, Based on the Common Core Standards

	6–8	9–12	
Common Core State Standards	CCSS.MATH. CONTENT.6.SP.A.1 Recognize a statistical question as one that anticipates variability in the data related to the question and accounts for it in the answers. (For example, "How old am I?" is not a statistical question, but "How old are the students in my school?" is a statistical question because one anticipates variability in students' ages.)	CCSS.MATH. CONTENT.HSS. ID.C.7 CCSS.MATH. CONTENT.HSS. ID.B.6 Represent data on two quantitative variables on a scatter plot, and describe how the variables are related.	CCSS.MATH. CONTENT.HSS. ID.B.5 Summarize categorical data for two categories in two-way frequency tables. Interpret relative frequencies in the context of the data (including joint, marginal, and conditional relative frequencies). Recognize possible associations and trends in the data.
Examples from the classrooms	Working in small groups, students sort 10 questions given to them in an envelope into two groups: statistical questions and nonstatistical questions.	Working in partners, students graph their data from the statistical table. From the graph, students write a sentence describing how the variables are related.	Working independently, students read a statistical table and write a paragraph interpreting the data. Students write a paragraph summarizing a trend found in the data.

HOW CAN DISCIPLINARY LITERACY BE USED WITH INQUIRY-BASED LEARNING?

Over the past generation, teaching has shifted from the "sage on the stage" who lectures to impart knowledge to students to the "guide on the side" who facilitates student-centered learning where students construct knowledge through new experiences, investigations, and projects. In the discipline of science, *inquiry-based learning* became the umbrella term to describe student-centered learning led by the students themselves. We say that inquiry-based learning is student-led because unlike traditional laboratory experiments where the teacher has determined the research questions to be investigated, the students ask the research questions and design the inquiry with the teacher's guidance and expertise (Buck Institute for Education, 2019).

Embedded within explicit instruction is the developmental theory of Vygotsky (1978) that emphasizes the social nature of cognition and learning. Vygotsky posits that the process of expanding cognition is best achieved through social interactions or "shared meaning" between instructor and learner. Over time, the cognitive processes of the instructor are internalized by the learner and reappear in the learner's thinking. The distance between the point where the learner initially functions with a task and the point of potential development as determined through support from an instructor or more capable peers is referred to as the *zone of proximal development*. Wood, Bruner, and Ross (1976) referred to this same process as *scaffolding*, connoting the notion of the instructor providing a support (that is, a scaffold) for the learner until the learner is capable of operating at a higher level without support. Metaphorically, the scaffold is removed and the learner has learned what is needed to be successful within a specific learning context.

Reflect: What does the scaffolding process with disciplinary literacy look like in your classroom?

We suggest using inquiry-based learning to apprentice students toward mastery of content as disciplinary insiders. Combining disciplinary literacy and inquiry provides students with the opportunity to engage in authentic learning by participating in the intellectual process that experts in the disciplines use to answer questions. Inquiry-based learning is authentic work (Bruner, 1960; Dewey, 1927) because it is relevant to real life and is inspired by real-world problems, and because final products are shared with real audiences. In our experience, when inquiry-based learning is combined with disciplinary literacy, the students' end products demonstrate deeper learning. The skills and knowledge that students gain from this process have value both in school and in students' everyday lives (Galileo Educational Network, 2017; Wilhelm, 2007). Combining disciplinary literacy with inquiry emphasizes both the process and the product of learning. Spires, Kerkhoff, and Graham (2016) note:

> When students address real-world problems that interest them, they are more likely to interact with information inquisitively and curiously, leading to authentic learning outcomes. We value disciplinary depth because deep disciplinary knowledge is a prerequisite for addressing complex issues. (p. 159)

Inquiry-based learning, however, is not without its critics; Mayer (2004) contends that teachers must provide guided support as students learn new information. Without thoughtful guided support, students may experience too much frustration, even cognitive overload (Sweller, 1988). We have all conducted lessons where we provided students with choices but then did not provide enough instructional scaffolding for the lesson to be successful. The products of learning, then, are not fully developed, and students often feel overwhelmed and disengaged from the lesson. Inquiry requires a cultural shift in the classroom for teachers and for the students. Teachers have to trust that their students will engage and persevere through the process; students have to trust that their teachers will reward their efforts and appreciate their creativity. The best way for teachers to create the cultural shift is simply to begin, and remain prepared to learn along the way—knowing there will be fits and starts.

Disciplinary inquiry allows students to engage in deep learning and knowledge creation within a discipline. The process is exemplified by the Revised Bloom's Taxonomy (Anderson & Krathwohl, 2001; see Figure 1.3) in which *create* is placed at the top of the triangle, indicating that cognitive processes in the lower portion of the triangle, such as remembering and understanding, are used in service of the creation process. Adding to this idea, we modified the Revised Bloom's Taxonomy to make *create* the largest section, because the ultimate goal of disciplinary inquiry is that students spend more time constructing and creating new information within a specific discipline (Spires, Wiebe, Young, Hollebrands, & Lee, 2009).

Figure 1.3. Revised and Inverted Bloom's Taxonomy

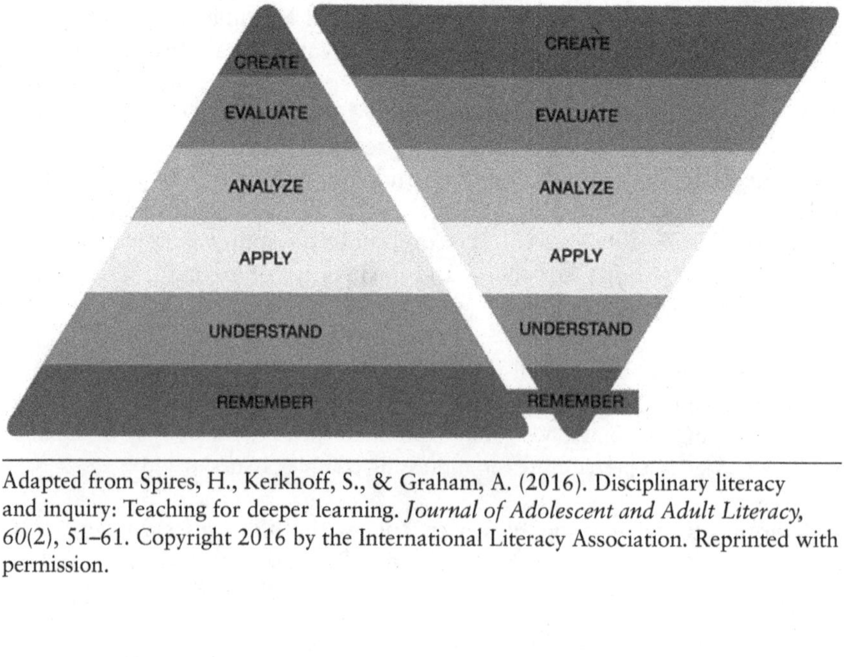

Adapted from Spires, H., Kerkhoff, S., & Graham, A. (2016). Disciplinary literacy and inquiry: Teaching for deeper learning. *Journal of Adolescent and Adult Literacy,* 60(2), 51–61. Copyright 2016 by the International Literacy Association. Reprinted with permission.

Seeing the prominent status of *create* helps us understand the role inquiry can play within our classrooms. It is important to note that we are not dismissing the key roles of remembering and understanding information. These cognitive processes are essential in the learning process. But in the Information Age, it is more important to know what to do with information than just to remember it. With access to search engines, we don't have to remember facts the way we had to before Google.

SUMMARY

This chapter provided foundational ideas about disciplinary literacy and inquiry, which are important as we move deeper into how to incorporate related practices with your students. At its foundation, disciplinary literacy makes explicit the special ways reading, writing, and inquiry take place in the disciplines. Though inquiry in each discipline has its own nuances, the goal is the same: to create new knowledge. When students are engaged in disciplinary literacy and inquiry, they are doing more than reading comprehension exercises; they are using literacy strategies to construct meaning in the context of a disciplinary problem or issue. In the next chapter, we explain a specific inquiry-based learning approach that we refer to as the Project-Based Inquiry (PBI) Model. The model includes disciplinary literacy strategies that align with the different phases of the PBI Model.

Now It's Your Turn!

At the end of each chapter, we will provide you with the steps to design your own PBI. Begin thinking about an overarching topic from your curriculum that you want to develop a lesson or unit around.

Questions to guide your brainstorming of topics:

1. What topic do you find challenging to teach?
2. What topic in your curriculum deserves a deeper dive?
3. What topic connects to a social justice issue in your community?
4. What topic connects to an important current event?

CHAPTER 2

Relating Disciplinary Literacy to Inquiry Through the Project-Based Inquiry (PBI) Model

Tell me and I will listen. Show me and I will see. Let me experience and I will learn.

—Laozi, Chinese philosopher

Centuries ago, Laozi understood the importance of experience as a key feature of the learning process. In the early 20th century, John Dewey (1916/2004) took the idea further, asserting that educators should "Give the pupils something to do, not something to learn" (p. 148). These early ideas are foundational to our contemporary notion of inquiry in schools.

Creating conditions for students to experience deep content learning requires involving students in their own learning process. Though *inquiry-based learning* is the term often heard in science education, other disciplines describe authentic, student-led learning experiences with terms such as *project-based learning*, *problem-based learning*, *design-based learning*, *challenge-based learning*, and *discovery learning*. All these terms describe a similar educational approach, but how the process begins, or the steps students take during the process, may vary. In this chapter, we explore in detail the PBI Model and explain how it can be applied practically in the classroom within different disciplines.

THE PBI MODEL

We use a unique inquiry model that we have termed *Project-Based Inquiry* (PBI). The PBI Model combines inquiry, which foregrounds authentic work, with disciplinary literacy practices, which foreground apprenticeship of reading, writing, and thinking in the disciplines. The PBI Model has been adapted from previous work we have done through the Massive Open Online Course (MOOC) for educators (Spires, Kerkhoff, Graham, & Lee,

2014), the New Literacies Teacher Leader Institute, and the New Literacies and Global Learning graduate degree program directed by the first author, Hiller Spires, at North Carolina State University.

See Figure 2.1 on pp. 24–25 for a visual demonstration of the PBI process integrated with four disciplines: English language arts (ELA), science, history/social studies, and mathematics. The following sections will break down this graphic and explain each phase in detail.

Ask a Compelling Question

Inquiry begins with a compelling question. The question must be provocative and open-ended, and must pique students' curiosity, compelling students to find an answer. Ideally, compelling questions should be relevant to students' interests and lives, and of social importance, which can make the inquiry process all the more engaging. We recommend that students generate their own questions, but we suggest that teachers assist with the question design process to ensure questions of high quality that are pertinent to the learning standards teachers are required to address. In our experience, it works best when the teacher provides students with the overarching topic to be investigated and students work in groups of four to develop their compelling question. Examples of compelling questions include: What are some reasons for food insecurity in our community? and Why does one of the world's highest food-exporting countries still suffer from high malnutrition?

Prior to generating compelling questions, the teacher will activate and/or build students' background knowledge through a shared reading and lessons on a particular theme. For example, in one PBI we conducted at a high school in the southeastern United States with 10th-grade English teacher Ms. Glover, all students read *A Long Walk to Water* by Linda Sue Park. This provided the students with a shared reading experience based on a true story that highlighted the global water crisis—the lack of clean water—as it manifested in South Sudan, Africa. In Table 2.1 on pp. 26–27, we illustrate how Ms. Glover applied PBI in her English class using the theme of the global water crisis. We also illustrate how the process could be applied to the disciplinary areas of ELA, science, history/social studies, and mathematics.

Students should work in partners or teams throughout PBI. We recommend grouping students by similar interests to give students the opportunity to explore a question that is of interest to them and at the same time to develop collaboration skills as they conduct their inquiry.

Compelling questions will often begin with *how* or *why*, which will facilitate the creation of an original product. We have developed an instructional process to guide question generation. During this process, the teacher models appropriate compelling questions that meet the criteria seen in Figure 2.2 on p. 28. The teacher provides the criteria for compelling questions to students in a PBI rubric and coaches students using the rubric

Figure 2.1. Relating Disciplinary Literacy to Project-Based Inquiry

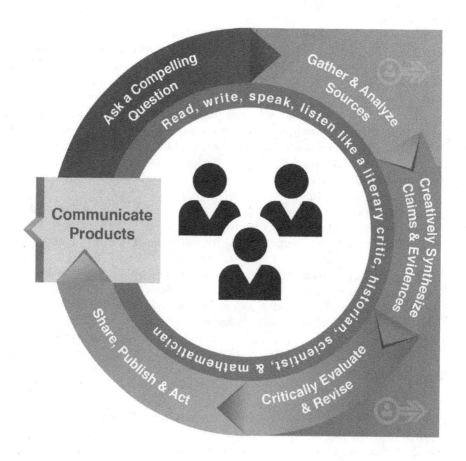

From Spires, H. A., Kerkhoff, S. N., Graham, A. C. K., & Lee, J. K. (2014). *Relating inquiry to disciplinary literacy: A pedagogical approach* (p. 2). Raleigh, NC: Friday Institute of Educational Innovation, North Carolina State University. Copyright 2014 by the Friday Institute of Educational Innovation, North Carolina State University. Reprinted with permission.

Figure 2.1. Relating Disciplinary Literacy to Project-Based Inquiry (continued)

LITERARY CRITIC	SCIENTIST	HISTORIAN	MATHEMATICIAN
• Read sources, e.g., novels, poems, short stories, essays. • Differentiate speaker from author point of view. • Deconstruct literacy & rhetorical devices, e.g., irony, symbolism, voice & style.	• Read original research sources, e.g., lab reports, scientific journal articles, graphs. • Determine author's credentials & authority within the field. • Understand phenomena, technical terms, essential characteristics, & abstract concepts.	• Read relevant information from historical sources, e.g., letters, photographs, maps. • Analyze sources focusing on subject, author, purpose, & audience; determine author's bias. • Contextualize sources to determine when, where, & why sources were created.	• Read advanced textbooks & authentic texts involving symbolic notations, graphic representations, illustrations. • Analyze logic of argument; place less emphasis on authorship. • Understand precise mathematical meaning in terminology & concepts.
• Organize by theme. • Interpret through critical lens, e.g., feminist, historical, Marxist. • Construct personal, intertextual & global connections. • Construct claims for literary critique w/ textual evidence & close examiniation of language.	• Organize topically, e.g., physical, life, earth. • Interpret data & analyze relationships of variables, e.g., cause & effect, patterns, systems, functions. • Construct models & explanations to support scientific hypothesis or design solutions.	• Organize geographically or chronologically. • Corroborate by comparing evidence from sources to develop & strengthen claims. • Construct arguments about the past integrating evidence from multiple sources.	• Organize by escalating logic. • Interpret among sentences, symbolic notations, & graphics. • Construct viable arguments using abstract & quantitative reasoning. • Aim for convergence on solution.
• Determine if claims are supported w/ adequate textual evidence & elaboration. • Revise for coherence, style & voice. • Represent response in multiple formats, e.g., prose, multimedia.	• Reflect on own bias; convey objective attitude & informed skepticism; determine generalizability. • Revise for validity & replicability. • Represent response in multiple formats, e.g., prose, diagrams, models, equations, tables.	• Determine limitations of historical evidence in supporting claims. • Detect inconsistencies in evidence; revise for strength & credibility of claims. • Represent response in multiple formats, e.g., narrative, multimedia.	• Monitor by critically questioning logic & reasoning. • Revise for precision & accuracy. • Represent response in multiple formats, e.g., equations, diagrams, models.

Table 2.1. Applying the PBI Process with Different Disciplines Using the Theme of the Global Water Crisis

	English Language Arts (ELA)	Science	History/Social Studies	Mathematics
Build Background Knowledge	Read and discuss *A Long Walk to Water*.			
Ask a Compelling Question	How does the title *A Long Walk to Water* apply to both main characters' narratives?	How can local water sources become potable?	What is the role of water in the historical conflicts in South Sudan?	How do walking speed, distance, and weight of the water container factor into the time it takes for water-gathering in South Sudan?
Gather & Analyze Sources	• Identify quotes in the novel related to "walk" and "water" using sticky notes. • View videos of Salva, Nya, and Linda Sue Park to differentiate between author's and main characters' voices.	• Locate scientific reports about water pollution and water potability. • Conduct lab testing of water in school pond.	• Analyze maps, e.g., economic, political, topographical. • View documentary (*God Grew Tired of Us*) about the lost boys of Sudan. • Read primary documents (transcript of *I Kept Walking*) about Salva Dut.	• Calculate the speed Nya traveled to collect water based on distance and time for going and coming. • Determine the weight of the filled container she carried. Use the formula for volume and water density to determine the weight of the container in pounds.

Creatively Synthesize Claims & Evidence	• Interpret through critical lens—for example, of gender or postcolonialism. • Construct claims for literary analysis paper with textual evidence and interpretation of walking and water as symbols.	• Interpret results from lab to determine microbes present. • Explore scientific journal articles that discuss elimination process of dangerous microbes. • Sketch and label a model for a public service announcement (PSA) that illustrates the elimination process.	• Corroborate sources, e.g., the maps, documentary, primary document, and book. • Construct an argument detailing the relationship between water access and the First Sudanese Civil War in South Sudan.	• Compare the speed/distance Nya walked with the average reported speed/distance walked by women in Africa to get water. • Compare the weight of the filled container Nya carried each day with other containers used in Africa. • Write the equation and then graph time and distance there and time and distance back.
Critically Evaluate & Revise	• Check that appropriate textual quotes from the novel accompany each claim. • Revise for coherence of claims and evidence.	• Evaluate language used to ensure objective attitude and tone. • Ensure written report and model for PSA are aligned.	• Evaluate limitations and biases exhibited in source materials and proposed argument. • Contextualize events in a timeline to visually represent the argument.	• Monitor for errors in mathematical procedures. • Examine logic and reasoning of equation.
Share, Publish, & Act	Publish multimodal literary analysis paper.	Publish PSA.	Publish interactive timeline using a web-based medium.	Publish infographic with graphs and explanation of the equation.
	Hold a community-wide walk to raise money to help build a well in South Sudan.			

Figure 2.2. Criteria for Compelling Questions

Compelling questions should:	• Be something you are motivated and curious about • Be of social importance • Line up with topic you are studying
Compelling questions should not:	• Be direct questions with direct answers • Be answered with a yes or no • Be unresearchable
Student team revision process of compelling question:	• 1st attempt: Is our city's water quality good or bad? • 2nd attempt: What are the effects of city growth on our water quality? • 3rd attempt: How do growing urban areas affect water quality in surrounding ecosystems?

Adapted from Spires, H. Kerkhoff, S., & Graham, A. (2016). Disciplinary literacy and inquiry: Teaching for deeper learning. *Journal of Adolescent and Adult Literacy, 60*(2), 51–61. Copyright 2016 by International Literacy Association. Reprinted with permission.

throughout the process. The teacher provides feedback as student teams brainstorm ideas to help them generate questions that will compel them to dig deep as they develop answers. Then, student teams share compelling questions for peer feedback, with the teams revising each compelling question until it meets the criteria.

Reflect: How can you revise a yes-no question to become a compelling question?

Gather and Analyze Sources

Once students' compelling questions have been decided, teachers can instruct students on how to gather and analyze sources. For example, a teacher may provide mini-lessons on how to conduct a web search productively, including keyword generation, Boolean search strategies, choosing the most relevant sources, and evaluating a website's credibility. The students must pay continuous attention to the relevance and credibility of sources during this phase, which can be particularly difficult for students. Research has shown that students often lack the critical-examination skills required for Internet research (Coiro, 2003; Leu, Kinzer, Coiro, & Cammack, 2004).

Students then gather digital and print resources that help them answer their compelling question. In addition to sources available online, students can collect their own data through experiments, interviews, and surveys. For example, when researching the question "What are some reasons for food insecurity in our community?," students interviewed experts at a local nonprofit who worked on hunger issues in the county. When investigating the compelling question of "With which Shakespearean character do seniors at our school most identify?," students created and distributed a Google Forms survey to their classmates.

Below, we explain the skills disciplinary experts in ELA, science, history/social studies, and mathematics use to gather and analyze sources during inquiry. For each discipline, we provide an example of how students employ disciplinary skills to complete a PBI utilizing *A Long Walk to Water* and the global water crisis.

ELA. As it is taught in secondary schools, English encompasses an integration of different disciplines: literary criticism, literary theory, linguistics, language arts, creative writing, composition, rhetoric, journalism, and communications. Expert readers within ELA primarily use what we call expressive literacy (Spires, Kerkhoff, Graham, Thompson, & Lee, 2018), meaning that they pay particular attention to how authors use language to express meaning. Unlike in the other three disciplines, in which the speaker is the same person as the author, readers differentiate between the speaker and the author.

The complexity of literature is created by layering literal and figurative meanings and playing with language. To engage in disciplinary literacy in ELA, literary critics must understand the literal layer, or the setting, characters, and plot of the text. A literary critic then unearths layers of meaning through deconstruction of rhetorical and literary devices, such as structure, style, voice, irony, figurative language, and symbolism. The deepest layer involves uncovering social commentaries or themes. Literary critics must read closely and often engage in repeated readings, combing over the text several times. Because each reader constructs an interpretation that goes below the factual layer in the text, individual readers may construct different interpretations of a text.

For the PBI on the global water crisis outlined in Table 2.1, students assumed the role of literary critics. Students discussed the setting of *A Long Walk to Water* and how the plot developed over the course of the novel. They then determined how the theme of the book constituted a social commentary on the issue of clean water access in South Sudan. Students also explored the complex characters presented in the book through the lens of feminist literary criticism to better understand how issues such as gender and status, along with lack of water access, prevent certain groups (for example, young impoverished girls) from participating in society in certain ways (for example, attending school). The information obtained from these discussions about the book was used to support students' answers to their compelling questions.

Students also viewed videos of Salva and Nya, the real people upon whom the main characters were based, as well as the author, Linda Sue Park, to differentiate between the author's and the characters' voices, a complicated task because the novel is fictionalized but based on Salva's real life and written by Linda Sue Park. Students began to question how the author's perception of the events influenced her storytelling.

Science. The science department in secondary settings is usually devoted to the natural sciences disciplines: life science, physical science, and Earth and space science. Sometimes science in secondary schools also includes the discipline of engineering. Across these disciplines, experts in science choose texts based on relevance of the topic to their area of research and the credibility of the text's author—or, if the author is unknown, the author's affiliated institution. For example, a text from a professor at MIT would be considered a credible source because MIT is a highly respected institution for science. Scientists use texts to build background knowledge and to identify gaps in knowledge that help them develop hypotheses. While reading articles, scientists utilize their knowledge of technical and quantitative terminology and traverse prose, diagrams, tables, and figures to build understanding (Cervetti & Pearson, 2012).

Scientific discourse uses language that implies degrees of certainty and is often subtle because science cannot prove that something is true, only that something is *not* true. For example, scientists often write phrases such as "results confirm that" to imply more certainty and "results suggest that" to imply a likely result but with less certainty. For this reason, expert readers in science pay close attention to the wording of information to appropriately interpret the author's findings.

The reading of *A Long Walk to Water* prompted chemistry students to explore the idea of "clean" water. Students conducted experiments in which they tested water from different ponds and rivers near their school to evaluate their potability. To take this examination further, one group wanted to better understand the chemicals and microbes that should and should not be in safe drinking water. The students then gathered scientific sources describing safe drinking water and the amounts of chemicals and microbes that can exist in it. Another group also explored how to make nonpotable water potable using natural resources such as stones.

History/Social Studies. Social studies in secondary schools comprises social sciences (for example, psychology, sociology, political science) and economics, as well as the humanities (such as history, religion, and philosophy). Reading and writing in social sciences can vary widely from reading and writing in the humanities.

Historians primarily utilize what we call *source literacy* (Spires et al., 2018). Based on Wineburg's (1991) seminal work, source literacy means that readers pay attention to the source of the information and the context surrounding the creation of the information. In history and social studies, who said something and why they said it is as important as what was actually said. Readers must identify who was reporting information and the biases the person had, as well as contextualize the text by understanding the surrounding events and conditions under which a text was authored. Experts in history analyze text to discover an author's intentions, biases, and motivations. To create a claim, they also read texts to corroborate information with other texts they have read. Historians often use the SCIM-C method (Hicks, Doolittle, & Ewing, 2004)—which stands for *summarize, contextualize, infer, monitor,* and *corroborate*—to explain how reading, writing, listening, and speaking are entwined with inquiry.

After reading *A Long Walk to Water,* students studied the history of South Sudan in their social studies classes. They explored the conflicts of the past century in the area and how access to clean water was one cause of the conflicts. To gather information, students analyzed economic, political, and topographical maps to understand more about the area of South Sudan. Students viewed the documentary *God Grew Tired of Us,* which told the story of the lost boys of Sudan and featured the main character in *A Long Walk to Water,* Salva Dut. Lastly, students read a transcript of *I Kept Walking,* a video about Salva Dut's experience. This transcript served as a primary document that provided a personal account of the conflict in Sudan.

Mathematics. Mathematicians employ a complex process of reading sentences, symbols, and graphics, which we refer to as analytical literacy (Spires et al., 2018). Mathematical texts include dense technical language and symbolic mathematical notation. For this reason, reading in mathematics requires deconstructing technical syntax and translating symbols to make meaning. Symbolic notations can stand for a number (π), unknown number (x), concept (∞), operation ($+$), or function (Σ). Mathematical texts also include quantitative graphs with little redundancy in words, so readers must make meaning across modes. For mathematicians, the source of the information is not as important as the clarity and accuracy of the answer to a problem (Hillman, 2014).

While gathering and analyzing sources, students at the high school had to look up information regarding distance and time, as well as formulas.

Using the numbers provided by the text and their research, students calculated the distance the main characters in *A Long Walk to Water* traveled each day to bring potable water to their village. Students also calculated the weight of the container. Students had to use the formula for volume and water density to determine how much the container would weigh in pounds.

Reflect: How can you utilize source literacy in domains other than history?

Creatively Synthesize Claims and Evidence

This phase of the inquiry process involves students generating claims that help answer their compelling question, a process that involves the higher levels of the Revised Bloom's Taxonomy (Anderson & Krathwohl, 2001). To generate claims, students consider the information gathered by critically examining both sides of an argument. They compare and contrast the details, looking for patterns to create a claim.

During this phase, literary critics and mathematicians are making sure their claims are plausible; both of these types of experts rely on logic to make arguments. Students then go back to the information to make sure there is strong evidence to support their claims. Historians and scientists, however, are using the process of corroboration by checking to see if their claims can be supported by multiple sources.

The types of sources used as evidence depend on the discipline as well as the compelling question. For example, a historian might use photographs and newspaper quotes to serve as evidence for a claim, while a scientist might use the results of a lab experiment or evidence from previous research. Just like the experts, students must justify their claims with evidence and articulate their reasoning for making such claims, a skill emphasized in state and national standards such as the Common Core State Standards (National Governors Association Center for Best Practices & Council of Chief State School Officers, 2010).

Following the generation and justification of claims, students employ creative synthesis—a design process that creates an original representation detailing students' inquiry results. The creative synthesis requires students to employ complex critical thinking within the disciplines through inferential reasoning, summarization of the most important ideas, and complex understanding, all while they design creative final products. The type of final product depends on the project and the discipline, and can even be an interdisciplinary endeavor across lines of inquiry. For example, students can design a historical website detailing the Native American nations that once lived where the students now call home, or create an interdisciplinary video explaining the design of a product, their calculations and reasonings for solving the problem the way they did, and the social significance of their new product in the real world.

The multimodal production process requires students to represent their information in creative ways. Students must utilize a variety of resources in a way that depicts the learning outcomes of the project in a technical and aesthetical manner (Spires, Hervey, Morris, & Stelpflug, 2012). To engage in the multimodal production process, students need to write text and select images or modes that illustrate their ideas, such as a video, an infographic, or a graphic website. In our digital society, audiences expect new knowledge to be depicted in visually compelling ways that may accompany print text. Students are challenged to represent their knowledge in a visually appealing way using digital tools. This is why we emphasize both the process and the product during PBI.

Below, we detail how experts from the four disciplines creatively synthesize claims and evidence and represent their synthesis. Again, we utilize examples from the PBI on the global water crisis.

ELA. Individual readers can interpret literary texts differently. As readers decode words, they also encode meaning into the text based on their experiences and prior knowledge. Readers read closely to uncover themes or social commentaries and may construct differing interpretations of texts (Galloway, Lawrence, & Moje, 2013).

However, to support any interpretation of a text, readers must be able to support their claims with evidence from the text, their life experiences, and literary theory. The synthesis of information may come from using multiple quotes from one novel, quotes from multiple works by the same author, quotes from multiple works of the same stylistic period, or quotes from different literary theorists to support a claim. For example, if an expert is making a claim that August Wilson's plays changed in complexity over time, quotes from different plays across Wilson's lifespan would be needed as evidence.

Tenth-grade students generated claims about the motif of water in *A Long Walk to Water* and supported their claims with quotes from the book. As students dove deeper and analyzed the symbolism of water from the perspective of both the girl and the boy main characters, they supported their claims with ideas from feminist literary criticism. Students made claims based on ideas from class discussions and pulled quotes from the novel and literary theory as evidence of their interpretation.

Science. Synthesis in science involves replication, or looking across several studies to validate theories and results of scientific processes. Scientists begin their inquiry process by reading to learn about what other scientists have discovered, and then creatively synthesize the information they read to form an original hypothesis. After conducting an experiment to test their hypothesis, scientists compare their findings with previously published studies. By synthesizing their claims with others' claims, scientists can establish a consensus and verification of their findings.

Students must also synthesize information when they conduct inquiries in science. One way students can conduct PBI is to read texts authentically to learn about others' inquiries about the natural world and creatively synthesize information to reach scientific consensus. Another way is for students to conduct experiments and then compare their firsthand experiments with previously published studies. In addition to synthesizing multiple texts when reading, students must be able to do so when writing, including representing data in tables and models and explanations of phenomena using words and images.

After conducting experiments on the potability of local water sources, students compiled their lab results with other scientific sources they had gathered into their claims and evidence. After researching the chemicals and microbes that should not be in safe drinking water, students explored other scientific journal articles that discussed the process of eliminating dangerous microbes to create a claim and evidence regarding how nonpotable water can be made clean. Then, students began to design a storyboard for a public service announcement (PSA), which would explain the issue of water potability as well as how microbes can be eliminated from polluted water sources.

History/Social Studies. Historians compile evidence from a variety of historical sources to develop a logical argument about events in the past. To develop the argument, historians must explore multiple accounts of past events to discover which aspects of the events are described consistently across multiple sources. In history, two terms are used to describe historians' work as they develop their claims and evidence: *corroboration* and *synthesis*. Though the processes are similar, corroboration is used to confirm which aspects of an event occurred, while synthesis is used to combine information from multiple sources to tell the story.

The historical analysis of South Sudan allowed students to develop their claims on the role clean water access has had in the nation's past conflicts. Students used reliable websites and personal narrative as evidence. By corroborating multiple historical accounts, along with information from Salva, students were able to develop a timeline and logical argument about how lack of access to clean water contributed to ethnic conflict in South Sudan.

Mathematics. Mathematicians read multiple sources to identify patterns, verify answers, and help explain their reasoning. Quantitative literacy enables mathematicians to think mathematically, which is different from being able to calculate numbers. Reading, writing, and thinking like a mathematician enables students to learn how to navigate the demanding language of the discipline across words, quantitative graphs, and symbols. Once students understand quantitative language and mathematical reasoning, they can develop a deeper conceptualization of mathematics.

Students used the mathematical calculations they performed to develop claims and evidence about how distance, time, and weight affect water transport in East Africa. Students detailed their calculations and equation on an infographic using graphs as visual representations of their numbers and sentences explaining their reasoning.

Critically Evaluate and Revise

In the fourth phase of the PBI cycle, students examine their claims and evidence and revise them. Often, students must reconsider their logic and/or add supporting evidence where required. For example, literary critics can revise their claims to be stronger by searching for disproving evidence to pose as a counterargument. Mathematicians can read their writing closely to evaluate the terminology used and revise it to make their argument clearer.

Although students can evaluate their own claims and evidence, peers and external experts can also be included in the evaluation. Ultimately, the three levels of evaluation—self, peer, and external—should use the same rubric that identifies both the intellectual and aesthetic goals of the project. The goals should be determined by what is valued in the discipline as well as the teacher's instructional objectives. The rubric used for this phase can be teacher-generated or student-generated or created with the teacher's and students' collaboration. After each level of evaluation, students revise their claims and evidence and creative products according to the feedback they receive. We'll discuss this process further in Chapter 5.

ELA. Revising in ELA occurs in two ways. First, students must evaluate the evidence they have provided and revise it to be stronger by deleting quotes that are not relevant to the claim and adding quotes where more evidence is needed. Second, students can revise stylistically to match their voice with their intended audience. Revising in this way involves examining and altering word choice and sentence structure, among other language arts considerations.

When revising their literary analysis on *A Long Walk to Water*, students were asked to examine specific quotes that they had chosen from the text. Often, students had to consider whether the quote actually related to and supported their argument, or if they could use a better quote. Students also edited their work to ensure that their claims and evidence were coherent and revised to include transitions where needed.

Science. In science, a text is evaluated based on the explanation of the methods used to test the hypothesis, such as the procedures, analyses, and claim construction. The methods must be explained consistently and thoroughly, yet concisely. When writing for other scientists, experts revise their writing to be thorough yet concise to allow replicability by readers and to increase the validity of their claims. When writing for the public as an audience, scientists revise to avoid jargon and to include definitions of scientific terminology.

Students revised their written lab reports, detailing the findings of their experiments to be clear to a wide variety of readers—in particular, those who may not be familiar with scientific terms. Also, students had to ensure that their claims and evidence were consistent and logical.

History/Social Studies. Creating claims in history is an iterative cycle. Experts in history must constantly look for new evidence and compare it with their claims. They must also examine their own assumptions and biases. Historians continually look for inconsistencies and revise their claims to increase credibility.

During the revision of their timelines, students were prompted to examine their personal biases and opinions. Students had to distance their assumptions from the actual historical information they were trying to present. During revisions, students examined their narratives to uncover inconsistencies or gaps in the narrative they had developed about the impact of clean water access on local conflicts.

Mathematics. Mathematicians must question the logic of their argument and critically revise their work to be more precise and concise. The goal in mathematics is to achieve precision and certainty with a single, defensible answer. To achieve this goal, mathematicians must revise their word choice to ensure that they convey the precise relationship or operation.

When reviewing their claims and evidence, students had to rework the problems they were presenting to ensure that they converged on the same answers and that their words matched the steps in the calculation. They examined word choice and order of presentation to ensure clarity in their equations and results.

Share, Publish, and Act

The culminating phase of the PBI process requires students to share their learning products with their classmates, school, family, and extended community. Students can share their products by hosting a showcase and publishing on social media platforms such as Instagram or Twitter. Students can share lab results on sites such as Figshare (figshare.com) or on Goodreads (goodreads.com). Sharing inquiry products allows students to engage authentic audiences in an intellectual and personal manner beyond school. Furthermore, students are often motivated and put forth extra effort when they know others will see their products.

Social media also invites out-of-school literacies into the classroom. By sharing their products online, students invite diverse audiences, who bring multiple perspectives, to review their created knowledge and converse on new topics.

Moreover, the inquiry process allows students to utilize their new knowledge and engage with the diverse audiences through community service projects and advocacy. For example, in the PBI event on the global water crisis, students held a community-wide walk to raise money to help build a well in South Sudan. (See the video that illustrates students discussing the project, including the showcase, the walk, and how they raised funds for a well in South Sudan: youtube.com/watch?v=yThjYHz3rhM&t=) Students were able to share their disciplinary products with other students and teachers at their school, as well as administrators, parents, and community members. Students were also motivated to use their new knowledge to convince community members of the urgency of donating funds to help build the well.

Reflect: Why is it important for your students
to engage with an authentic audience?

SUMMARY

The PBI Model provides teachers with a framework to plan and implement inquiry-based learning in their classes. By intentionally combining disciplinary literacy and inquiry, the PBI process engages students with creating knowledge that they can share with the community and the world. As Dewey said, "It is not enough to have a map in hand; we need to have made the journey" (quoted in Bomer & Bomer, 2001, p. 155). Inquiry as a pathway for better understanding societal issues can result in a participatory approach to learning. When students pose compelling questions around their interests, they become engaged in the journey of dialogue and constructing new knowledge in a discipline, and they become more engaged in developing claims and evidence that answer their question. The PBI process allows for disciplinary distinctions during the Gather and Analyze Sources, Creatively Synthesize Claims and Evidence, and Critically Evaluate and Revise phases, helping students develop discipline-specific skills. Sharing student products in the final phase of Share, Publish, and Act both motivates students to do their best work and invites the community to engage with students on what they are learning at school.

Now It's Your Turn!

You can download a sample of a PBI for each discipline from the online sources below. These lessons are also included in print at the end of this book in Appendices A–D.

📖 **English/Language Arts**—tinyurl.com/PBIDLELA

🧪 **Science**—tinyurl.com/PBIDLScience

🌐 **History/Social Studies**—tinyurl.com/PBIDLhistory

📦 **Mathematics**—tinyurl.com/PBIDLmath

Now you can begin planning your PBI. We will scaffold the process for you by focusing on one phase of the project in each chapter. In Chapter 1, you began thinking of a topic for your project to use with your students. At this point, you will turn your topic into a compelling question. As you design your PBI, you can use our online Lesson Plan Template, which can be found at tinyurl.com/DLPBItemplate. This template is also included in print at the end of the book in Appendix E.

Ask a Compelling Question

High-quality inquiry demands questions that compel us to seek an answer. In part, compelling questions emerge from our interests. In other words, we are most naturally compelled by things that are important to us. A compelling question should also be an invitation to learn more. The more open-ended and provocative, the better the question for inquiry. Compelling questions should be authentic. In fact, the sense of authenticity can be the most compelling aspect of inquiry. Make sure the answer to your question can be constructed. In other words, you should not be able to Google the answer to the question. Rather, through a thoughtful process of inquiring, students will design the answer to the question based on multiple resources and reflections.

Examples of Compelling Questions by Discipline

📖 **ELA:** What makes a good argument?

🧪 **Science:** What are the costs and benefits of genetic engineering?

🌐 **History/Social Studies:** How did problems associated with the Electoral College impact recent presidential elections in the United States?

📦 **Mathematics:** What cellphone plan is best for my family?

Based on your chosen topic, write your own compelling questions that could guide inquiry in your discipline. Although you may choose to have your students generate their own questions, it's good to have a few possible suggestions planned in advance.

CHAPTER 3

Gathering and Analyzing Sources

Getting Close to Close Reading

Some books should be tasted, some devoured, but only a few should be chewed and digested thoroughly.

—Francis Bacon

As we've discussed, our PBI Model requires the learner to ask a compelling question; gather and analyze sources; creatively synthesize claims and evidence; critically evaluate and revise; and finally, share, publish, and act. When students gather and analyze sources for PBI, we suggest that they conduct a close reading of at least one text. In this chapter, you will learn more about how to support your students as they gather and analyze online sources and conduct close readings to dive deeper into disciplinary learning.

GATHER AND ANALYZE ONLINE SOURCES

Before addressing close reading, we need to discuss how students can gather the sources they will analyze in close reading. Because students usually turn to the Internet to locate sources, they must learn how to conduct effective online searches and determine which sources provide high-quality information.

Although today's students are often familiar with online search engines, in our experience, they don't always know the best terms to use when searching. To prepare students for searching online, you may want to help them brainstorm keywords that relate to their topic and consider synonyms, long-tail keywords, and multiple ways of phrasing sentences they want to search. Offering students a brief tutorial on Boolean search engines may help as well. For example, students may need to know that if they write a phrase in quotation marks in the search box, the search engine will look for that phrase—exactly as it is worded—on websites and in articles. Showing students a video like Code.org's *The Internet: How Search Works* (youtube. com/watch?v=LVV_93mBfSU) can be a good place to begin.

You can also work in regular mini-lessons to help your students learn how to use search engines effectively. We recommend using A Google a Day (agoogleaday.com). In this daily challenge, a question is provided, along with tips and tricks for finding the answer. Students are able to search using Google. The faster a student finds the answer, the more points he or she will receive! Using this tool in your classroom can allow students to hone their online searching skills while engaging in a game.

If you prefer not to allow your students to have full access to the web through Google, try search engines designed for younger students, such as Kiddle (kiddle.co), KidRex (alarms.org/kidrex), or KidzSearch (kidzsearch .com). For older students, turn on Google SafeSearch (fosi.org/good-digital -parenting/how-activate-google-safe-search).

Once students have learned how to conduct effective searches for sources online, they must learn how to examine the sources for credibility and accuracy. When conducting PBI, we use the CRAAP test, which helps students assess sources for *currency, relevance, authority, accuracy,* and *purpose* (see csuchico.edu/lins/handouts/eval_websites.pdf).

Each step of the CRAAP test has questions for students to consider. For example, to assess the currency of an article, students must examine the article's publication date, investigate whether the information contained in the article has been updated elsewhere, consider whether their topic requires new information or if traditional sources will suffice, and test all links to see if they are functional. The test for relevancy helps students determine whether the information in the article will help them obtain the material needed for their research. In examining authority, students test whether the author and publisher of the article are reliable and credible. The most difficult parts of the CRAAP test are the last two steps, accuracy and purpose. In these steps, students must investigate whether the information is objective and unbiased—important 21st-century skills that will help students sift through the many sources of information on the Internet.

Similarly, Julie Coiro (2014) suggests that students' ability to make reasoned judgments about the quality of web-based information depends on their clear understanding of the following four elements: (1) the relevance of the text to the reading purpose, (2) the factual accuracy of the text, (3) the author's perspective when crafting the text, and (4) the reliability of the text based on the author's and publisher's reputations.

After you define and discuss these elements with your students, encourage them to compare and contrast the terms so they will have a deep understanding of what each one means within the context of gathering and analyzing online sources. Additional time can be devoted to the disciplinary contexts for online information so that students are reading and thinking like a disciplinarian while simultaneously making judgments about the accuracy and credibility of the sources.

Once students have found high-quality sources, they are ready to begin a close reading of the information they have deemed current, relevant, and accurate.

Reflect: How can you help students prepare to search online,
and why is this important?

WHAT IS CLOSE READING?

Close reading became a popular topic in 2010, when it became part of the
Common Core State Standards. Though the term is common, the meaning
of *close reading* is not as clear as one might think. The act of close reading
originated in literature studies as early as the 1930s (Hinchman & Moore,
2013). Nowadays, close reading is performed in all subject areas, though
each subject has its own ways of close reading.

In general terms, close reading involves "engaging with a text of sufficient complexity directly and examining meaning thoroughly and method-
ically" (Partnership for Assessment of Readiness for College and Careers,
2011, p. 7). In other words, close reading requires the reader to focus in-
tensively on the text itself. As a result, readers must attempt to forget about
information that is not provided by the author. The act of close reading involves an interaction that occurs primarily between the reader and the text.

Readers must also interpret the text. For example, a reader must first
understand what the author is saying in the text. As part of understanding
a text, readers must understand how the text works—how authors' word
choice and text structure support and extend their ideas.

Disciplinary literacy skills are enacted during the interpretation of the
text. With a newspaper editorial, a close reading would involve examining
the editorial board's position, the evidence used in the argument, and the
structure and logic of the argument. A close reading of a scientific study
would entail understanding the hypothesis, the methods used to conduct the
experiment, and the findings of the experiment. Conducting a close reading
of a short story would require understanding the plot and investigating literary devices that the author uses to tell the story.

Close reading is important because, outside the classroom, 21st-century
readers often begin reading texts without significant prior knowledge or
adequate preparation for reading. They must negotiate meaning with the
text independently, without a teacher or other students to help them understand what the text means. Furthermore, readers must be able to understand how a text works, decipher the author's point of view, and critically
analyze the information in the text. These are essential 21st-century reading skills, and teachers must educate students on how to conduct close
readings of texts in all disciplines to be effective critical readers (Kerkhoff
& Spires, 2015).

Reflect: What processes comprise close reading in your classroom?

CLOSE READING IN THE DISCIPLINES

Reading disciplinary texts closely can be challenging and requires several different skills (Shanahan, Fisher, & Frey, 2012; Shanahan, Shanahan, & Misischia, 2011). Research on how disciplinary experts read has shown that these experts use different skills in different ways to read and analyze texts. For example, research has shown that historians examine the source of the text (for example, a newspaper article, a handwritten note, or a diary entry) as well as the author (Wineburg, 1991). Historians also seek out other sources of information to either corroborate or disagree with the information contained in a text. Mathematicians, however, often are not concerned with the identity of the author, but rather the logic and accuracy of the mathematical solution presented in a text (Shanahan, Shanahan, & Misischia, 2011). Scientists typically question whether a text corroborates their background knowledge and spend more time analyzing any graphics that are present within the text (Shanahan & Shanahan, 2008). And literary critics focus more on the author's word choice and the literary devices that are used in the text.

To clarify the differences between the disciplines in close reading, we provide examples of how disciplinary experts might conduct close readings of disciplinary texts. Quotes from the texts are provided in segments, followed by examples of the experts' thought process and text analysis. In essence, each expert did a think-aloud as they read and reflected on the text from a disciplinary perspective.

Close Reading in ELA

Let's consider how a literary critic might do a close reading of Abraham Lincoln's Gettysburg Address. Quotes from the speech are italicized, followed by the analysis that was conducted by Eric Broer, a high school English teacher.

> *Four score and seven years ago, our fathers brought forth on this continent, a new nation, conceived in liberty, and dedicated to the proposition that all men are created equal.*

A literary critic would examine the metaphors that Lincoln uses in this statement. The use of *fathers* and *liberty* shape the rest of his speech about the birth of a nation. These metaphors combine with the connotation of the word *conceived*, implying that these fathers, together with liberty, conceived the nation.

> *Now we are engaged in a great civil war, testing whether that nation, or any nation so conceived and so dedicated, can long endure. We are met on a great battlefield of that war.*

In this sentence, Lincoln switches tenses. He uses the present tense, stating "we are engaged" and "we are met on a great battlefield." A literary critic would also note his use of the plural pronoun *we* to indicate that the entire nation is on this battlefield and that the entire nation is engaged in a great civil war.

> We have come to dedicate a portion of that field, as a final resting place for those who here gave their lives that that nation might live. It is altogether fitting and proper that we should do this.

A literary critic would note that again, Lincoln uses the word *we* in "We have come to dedicate." Lincoln uses the word *nation* several times throughout his speech, implying that he believes the Union is strong and must remain strong. With the usage of the word *live* in the phrase "that the nation might live," Lincoln harkens back to the introductory message regarding the forefathers and liberty conceiving the nation.

> But, in a larger sense, we can not dedicate—we can not consecrate— we can not hallow—this ground. The brave men, living and dead, who struggled here, have consecrated it, far above our poor power to add or detract. The world will little note, nor long remember what we say here, but it can never forget what they did here. It is for us the living, rather, to be dedicated here to the unfinished work which they who fought here have thus far so nobly advanced. It is rather for us to be here dedicated to the great task remaining before us—that from these honored dead we take increased devotion to that cause for which they gave the last full measure of devotion—that we here highly resolve that these dead shall not have died in vain—that this nation, under God, shall have a new birth of freedom—and that government of the people, by the people, for the people, shall not perish from the earth.

A literary critic would notice that the last idea is expressed in one long sentence, broken up with dashes. Although this was initially given as a speech, Lincoln understood that it would be published and therefore read. The use of dashes allows him to indicate to his reading audience that those clauses within the dashes are of great importance. In those clauses, Lincoln stresses to his audience that "this nation, under God" is "of the people, by the people, for the people." In this section, once again, Lincoln refers to the understanding that liberty is what birthed the nation.

Close Reading in Science

Next, we explore how science education instructional coach Lindsay Lewis, reading like a scientist, conducted a close reading of a lab report. The excerpt used (in italics) is a sample report accessed on StudyLib (Factors That Affect the Activity of the Enzyme Catalase, n.d.).

The conclusion of the report states:

The results indicate that copper sulfate does inhibit catalase activity. The tube that contained hydrogen peroxide, liver and water without the presence of the inhibitor produced five centimeters of oxygen gas bubbles after one minute. The second tube which contained hydrogen peroxide, liver and the inhibitor only formed one centimeter of bubbles after one minute. Since there were fewer bubbles in tube 2, the hydrogen peroxide was broken down more slowly when the inhibitor was used. This indicates that the use of an inhibitor slows down enzyme activity and therefore, slows the rate of decomposition of hydrogen peroxide.

A scientist would recognize the first sentence as a claim: "The results indicate that copper sulfate does inhibit catalase activity." Followed by the claim are two pieces of evidence, which reveal that the tube with hydrogen peroxide, liver, and water, which did not have the inhibitor, produced 5 centimeters of oxygen gas bubbles after 1 minute. The second tube, which contained hydrogen peroxide, liver, and the inhibitor, formed only 1 centimeter of bubbles after 1 minute. A scientist would notice that the time it took the bubbles to form was the same, which would be a constant variable. These two pieces of evidence are then followed by reasoning. Because there were fewer bubbles in tube 2, the hydrogen peroxide was broken down more slowly when the inhibitor was used. This indicates that the use of an inhibitor slows down enzyme activity and therefore slows the rate of decomposition of hydrogen peroxide, and decomposition of hydrogen peroxide is the variable that was being measured.

Close Reading in History/Social Studies

For the history example, we use the Gettysburg Address again. Dr. Crystal Simmons, a professor of social studies education, reads the Gettysburg Address (in italics) like a historian. Note the difference in the close reading of the same text that was previously conducted by a literary critic. The text begins:

Four score and seven years ago, our fathers brought forth on this continent, a new nation conceived in liberty, and dedicated to the proposition that all men are created equal.

A historian would recognize that Lincoln mentions the year 1776 and might consider other information he or she has read about this passage. For example, the well-known historian Matthew Pinsker describes Lincoln as evoking a biblical certainty in his address (see youtube.com/watch?v=2E boYQXY4FA for his close reading of this text). The reader might question: What would make Lincoln so confident in his language? By investigating the context of the Gettysburg Address, or by having extensive background knowledge, a historian would realize that the Battle of Vicksburg was won on the same day as Gettysburg. As a result, Lincoln would have confidence in the Union Army winning the Civil War.

The next segment of the text reads:

> *Now we are engaged in a great civil war, testing whether that nation, or any nation so conceived and so dedicated, can long endure. We are met on a great battlefield of that war.*

A historian might note the lessening confidence of Lincoln in this statement, and connect it with the fact that the Battle of Gettysburg was a missed opportunity for the Union—General Meade did not pursue General Lee at Gettysburg. Historians often reference other source material to support their thoughts regarding a text, and a historian could refer to the letter Lincoln wrote to General Meade 8 days after the battle of Gettysburg, in which he stated: "Again, my dear general, I do not believe you appreciate the magnitude of the misfortune involved in Lee's escape. He was within your easy grasp and to have closed upon him would, in connection with our other late successes, have ended the war."

The Gettysburg Address continues:

> *We have come to dedicate a portion of that field, as a final resting place for those who here gave their lives that that nation might live. It is altogether fitting and proper that we should do this.*

As president of the Union, Lincoln's main focus is on preserving the Union at all costs. A historian would recall that Lincoln took a limited approach to abolition in the Emancipation Proclamation and was willing to cooperate with the South in Reconstruction.

> *But, in a larger sense, we can not dedicate—we can not consecrate— we can not hallow—this ground. The brave men, living and dead, who struggled here, have consecrated it, far above our poor power to add or detract. The world will little note, nor long remember what we say here, but it can never forget what they did here. It is for us the living, rather, to be dedicated here to the unfinished work which they who fought here have thus far so nobly advanced.*

Here, Lincoln is encouraging citizens to think of the ways they can further promote their pursuit of liberty and equality through civic duty and sacrifice. A historian might note that several presidents and leaders of the United States have asked citizens to do this as well. For example, Franklin Roosevelt famously said, "We have nothing to fear but fear itself." John F. Kennedy stated, "My fellow Americans, ask not what your country can do for you, ask what you can do for your country." And Jimmy Carter noted that "too many of us now tend to worship self-indulgence and consumption. Human identity is no longer defined by what one does, but by what one owns." A historian might also investigate whether, when other presidents have spoken in these terms, the situations were similar. For example, Roosevelt made his famous observation during the Great Depression, another dark time for U.S. citizens. Lincoln continues:

> It is rather for us to be here dedicated to the great task remaining
> before us—that from these honored dead we take increased devotion
> to that cause for which they gave the last full measure of devotion—
> that we here highly resolve that these dead shall not have died
> in vain—that this nation, under God, shall have a new birth of
> freedom—and that government of the people, by the people, for the
> people, shall not perish from the earth.

A historian might note the upturn here, in which Lincoln seeks to connect the death of soldiers with the success of the war and the prosperity of the Union. It is important to remember that the Gettysburg Address was published in the year leading up to the 1864 presidential election, in which Lincoln was running for reelection.

Close Reading in Mathematics

The excerpt of text (in italics) for the following close reading of mathematics, conducted by Dr. Erin Krupa, an associate professor of mathematics education, comes from Course 2 of the Core-Plus Mathematics textbook (Hirsch, Fey, Hart, Schoen, & Watkins, 2008, pp. 182–183, © 2008 by McGraw Hill).

> Drilling teams from oil companies search around the world for new
> sites to place oil wells. Increasingly, oil reserves are being discovered in
> offshore waters.

Upon reading this, a mathematician might immediately visualize these oil reserves. This is the beginning of mathematical modeling.

The text goes on to say:

The Gulf Oil Company has drilled two high capacity wells in the Gulf of Mexico, 5 kilometers and 9 kilometers from the shore. The 20 kilometers of shoreline is nearly straight and the company wants to build a refinery on shore between the two wells.

A mathematician might visualize these two oil refineries in the middle of the ocean, where one is 5 kilometers away from shore and the other is 9 kilometers away from shore. There are 20 kilometers of shoreline between them. The mathematician would recognize the goal of locating a refinery on the shore between the two wells, but the task cannot be accomplished yet because restrictions are not yet known. A mathematician might mathematically represent the two wells and the given distances and begin constructing models and representations based on the interpretation of the problem so far.

The next section of the text states:

Since pipe and labor costs money, the company wants to find a location that will serve both wells and uses the least amount of pipe when it is laid in straight lines from each well to the refinery.

At this point, more constraints enter the text: The problem is posed, which is that the company wants to save money on the pipe and labor needed to construct the refinery. A mathematician would read this as a desire to minimize the distance between the two wells and the refinery by having the refinery located between the two wells on the coastline. A mathematician might start with a pictorial representation of this scenario; the representations that each mathematician might come up with would be different.

The text goes on to ask:

How can coordinates be used to model the situation?

Depending on how the mathematician draws the mathematical model, the coordinates might vary. A mathematician would recognize that this is acceptable, as there is no singular answer to this question.

What distance should you try to minimize to use the least amount of pipe?

This question is about the distance between the wells, the refinery, and how much pipe it would take. A mathematician would want to minimize, and it would be important to understand that *minimize* means reducing the distance as much as possible.

The third question is:

Do you think the refinery should be closer to A, to B, or to midpoint of the shoreline? Make a conjecture.

A key tenet of mathematical literacy is making hypotheses and testing them, so at this point, the mathematician would make a conjecture and test it. The fourth question is:

Determine your best estimate for the location of the refinery. About how much pipe will be required?

At this point, the mathematician will begin to solve the problem. A mathematician would realize that there are several points of entry to begin solving this problem, as well as different methods for solving this problem, including analyzing tables or graphs of a function that relates to the total length of the pipeline and distance to the refinery. The multiple points of entry and multiple methods would cue the mathematician that this problem will have an algebraic solution.

Comparing the Close Readings in the Disciplines

These examples model how experts in ELA, science, history/social studies, and mathematics would conduct a close reading of a disciplinary text. A reader must utilize varying strategies and skills to understand and analyze the different texts. As seen in the Gettysburg Address example, a disciplinary expert in ELA focuses more on syntax and word choice to understand the authorial intent, whereas a history or social studies expert more closely examines dates, contextual information, source information, and corroborating material. Scientists most explicitly focus on the methods, procedure, and outcome of an experiment, using text structure to guide their understanding of the material. And mathematicians break the text apart and create mental models of the information, while examining specific words to ensure that the meaning of the text is understood as the author intended.

Reflect: Why is it important for students to know how to conduct a close reading within your discipline? Is this reason different in other disciplines?

CLOSE READING IN THE CLASSROOM

Learning to closely read and analyze disciplinary texts like an expert in a particular discipline is an important aspect of obtaining disciplinary literacy. For students to learn discipline-specific strategies and to conduct disciplinary close readings, however, teachers themselves must be well-versed in subject-specific strategies. Some teachers may struggle with how to teach disciplinary discourse to their students—especially when it comes to teaching this discourse through close reading.

We recommend that teachers conduct close readings during the second phase of PBI, Gather and Analyze Sources, and be aware of the following principles:

- Conducting a close reading of a text is challenging. Many students—especially reluctant readers—find it easier to talk about their experiences and feelings instead of their analysis of a text.
- Students will need opportunities during class to engage with challenging text. Teachers should not allow students to become overly frustrated; instead, they must find a balance between pushing students and exhausting them.
- Teachers must embrace close reading. Students often take cues from teachers' relationships with text. If the teacher demonstrates enthusiasm for reading challenging texts, talks about his or her own struggle for comprehension at times, and shares the belief that everyone can get better at reading, the students are more likely to develop the habit of close reading.

We recommend following these three steps to begin conducting close readings in the classroom:

1. Select a short text that is worthy of a close reading. Some texts are better than others. Think about Francis Bacon's quote at the beginning of this chapter. Make sure the text is one that is challenging and nuanced, or should be "chewed and digested thoroughly."
2. Model how to perform a close reading by thinking aloud and then inviting students to practice as they read silently. Students can alternate between reading silently and orally and thinking out loud with a partner.
3. Have students read and reread during the process. Many students enjoy slowing down and diving deep into a text. They will need scaffolds, though, so it is important for teachers to model close reading strategies, such as annotating.

STRATEGIES FOR CLOSE READING

Some content-area strategies that can facilitate close reading appear in Table 3.1. These strategies are general; they can be used across disciplines to help students read and respond to text.

Table 3.1. Content-Area Strategies for Close Reading

Strategy	Description	Example
Sentence Stems (Kerkhoff, 2014)	Students receive sentence stems that prompt them to write responses and summaries of texts.	On page . . . , the author says . . . I agree with the author when she says . . .
#Summaries	Using their digital literacy knowledge, students summarize each chunk of text by using a # and 1–4 words that summarize the main idea of that chunk.	#WhatBearsEat #CorporateWaterPollution #StarsMotif #SustainableDevelopment
GIST (Frey, Fisher, & Hernandez, 2003)	Stands for *Generating Interaction* between *Schemata* and *Text*. Students read a few sentences until they reach specified stopping points. At each point, vocabulary is discussed, the reading is explained, and students write a sentence summarizing what they read. At the end of the text, students have several summarizing sentences.	See bit.ly/2yVHBz6 for further explanation of the strategy and an example unit teaching the strategy.
Signposts (Beers & Probst, 2015)	Signposts are a way to signal readers when to slow down and close read in a text. There are six signposts for fiction and five for nonfiction that Beers and Probst identify as times good readers stop and ask themselves questions. Two examples of signposts are when something contrasts with what the reader expected and when something is repeated again and again in a text.	See the six signposts for fiction texts: bit.ly/2QJA0bd See the five signposts for nonfiction texts: bit.ly/2FpV8lJ

Moving from content-area strategies to disciplinary reading strategies can be difficult for both teachers and students. Utilizing a framework for instruction and a reading strategy to scaffold students during close reading of informational texts can make disciplinary close reading easier. Effective reading strategies allow for teacher modeling and gradual release of responsibility from the teacher to the student (McLaughlin, 2010), which provides opportunities for students to gain understanding of the author's craft and to have a reading strategy that can be used independently.

Table 3.2. Disciplinary Strategies for Close Reading

Strategy	Discipline	Example
TP-CASTT (IRA/NCTE, 2011)	ELA	bit.ly/29go4sd
TOADS (Kerkhoff, 2014)	Science	See Figure 3.1
SOAPSTone (College Board, 2004)	Science	bit.ly/2PSSpGe
SOAPSTone (College Board, 2004)	History/Social Studies	bit.ly/2PSSpGe
PPVV	Mathematics	See Figure 3.2

Disciplinary close-reading strategies can be seen in Table 3.2. The College Board (2004) promotes SOAPSTone (speaker, occasion, audience, purpose, subject, tone), a series of questions that students ask themselves, and then answer, as they read and write informational texts in social studies and history. The ReadWriteThink initiative of the National Council for Teachers of English promotes TP-CASTT (translate, paraphrase, connotation, attitude, shift, title, and theme) for close reading of poetry (see bit.ly/29go4sd).

Neither strategy targets the close reading of informational texts necessary for critical analysis of college and career texts and high-stakes assessments in science or mathematics. To meet this need, our second author, Shea Kerkhoff, created TOADS (title, organization, author's purpose, diction, summary) (Kerkhoff, 2014) to offer grade 6–12 teachers and students a framework for analyzing informational texts in science. TOADS becomes a reading strategy that is easy for students to remember when reading independently. Because TOADS can be modified for elementary and middle school students, it enables consistency in systemwide science literacy instruction in grades 6–12. Our second and third authors, Shea Kerkhoff and Casey Medlock Paul, designed PPVV (preview, predict, visualization, vocabulary) as a literacy strategy in mathematics. TOADS and PPVV strategies are outlined in Figures 3.1 and 3.2, respectively.

Students also use close reading to consider the author's craft and think about the decisions writers make when communicating to an audience. In addition to being dependent on an audience, craft choices are dependent upon discipline; students read closely to learn how writing in history is different from writing in science. In this way, students read to learn how to write in the discipline. Students can engage in disciplinary writing during the third phase of the PBI process, Creatively Synthesize Claims and Evidence, where they learn to write claims and evidence as well as represent them in visually compelling ways using digital formats.

Figure 3.1. TOADS (Title, Organization, Author's Purpose, Diction, Summary)

	TOADS for Close Reading in Science
Title	1. What do you predict the text will be about? Underline the key words in the title and as you continue to read.
Organization	2. What is the genre (research journal article, textbook, journalism, trade book)? How is the text structured? Are there text features to help (headings, charts, graphs, pictures, boldface words)?
	3. What is the author's organizational structure (chronological, order of importance, pro/con, cause/effect, problem/solution, compare/contrast)? Circle the transition words that signal how the text is organized.
	4. Circle the signal words that help in cohesion (and therefore in your reading comprehension).
	5. Is there a shift in genre or structure?
Author's Purpose	6. Mark facts (F) and opinions (O).
	7. What is the point of view (author's only, balanced and objective, multiple points of view)?
	8. What is the author's main purpose, written in a complete sentence (to persuade, to inform, to entertain, to describe)?
Diction	9. What words did you look up in the dictionary?
	10. What words have multiple meanings?
	11. Box words that illuminate the tone. What is the author's tone or attitude (optimistic, pessimistic, polite, insensitive, judgmental, matter-of-fact, sarcastic, sincere, formal, informal)? How does the author's word choice lead to tone?
	12. Does the author's word choice reveal biases?
Summary	13. Paraphrase the main idea. (Putting it in your own words requires more thought than just copying the main idea.)

Figure 3.2. PPVV (Preview, Predict, Visualization, Vocabulary)

PPVV for Close Reading in Mathematics	
Preview	Are there pictures?
	Charts?
	Graphs?
	Equations?
	Boldface words?
Predict	If there is a title, what is it? What do you predict the text will be about?
	Can you estimate? What do you think the solution might be?
Visualization	Visualize a mental model or draw the concepts in the text.
Vocabulary	Circle the key words that identify mathematical operations.
	Look up technical and quantitative words that you do not know in the glossary or dictionary.

Reflect: Which strategy are you most interested
in using with your students and why?

SUMMARY

In this chapter, we demonstrated how to conduct a close reading as a literary critic, scientist, historian, and mathematician. It is important to model close readings so students can conduct their own as they dive deeper into disciplinary learning. Students should have opportunities to practice close reading in a discipline before they are expected to be independent readers. Additionally, supporting your students as they gather and analyze sources for PBI requires critical and digital literacy. Making sure sources are credible and reliable requires critically questioning author authority and bias, which are critical literacy skills, and conducting Internet searches to find credible and reliable sources requires digital literacy. In the next chapter, we discuss in further detail critical and digital literacies and provide information on global literacy as well.

NOW IT'S YOUR TURN!

Now you will begin planning the Gathering and Analyzing Sources phase for your PBI with students. After students decide on a compelling question, they will use a wealth of print and digital resources to gather pertinent information to address their question. Notice that in the PBI Model, we have differentiated how experts (literary critics, scientists, historians, and mathematicians) in the four core disciplines gather and analyze sources during inquiry. It is important for the teacher to provide appropriate instruction in how to conduct productive web searches, taking into consideration key informational sites relative to a particular discipline. Students should pay particular attention to the credibility and reliability of information as they gather and analyze their sources.

Additionally, we suggest that students conduct at least one close reading of a source that they locate. The source they target for a close reading should be one that is challenging and nuanced, and thus worthy of a close-reading procedure. Online, you can watch an expert conduct a close reading by discipline:

English/Language Arts—youtube.com/watch?time_continue=4&v=xoPtpdMcNcc

Science—youtube.com/watch?v=v-2LcPPWRS4

History/Social Studies—youtube.com/watch?time_continue=4&v=xoPtpdMcNcc

Mathematics—youtube.com/watch?v=bdMtXk_DrtM&t

Now, choose a text for which you will model a close reading as part of your PBI lesson. Find the Lexile score to see if it is in the grade-level band of your class. Then, annotate the text or a portion of the text and record yourself close reading. Options you can think about using to capture your close reading are video, VoiceThread, Screencast-O-Matic, Jing, or Prezi. Refer back to the YouTube videos to listen to experts conduct a close reading of a disciplinary text. The purpose of conducting your own close reading is so you will have a model to share with your students.

CHAPTER 4

Creatively Synthesizing Information

Building Digital and Global Literacies

We are obliged to know we are global citizens.

—Maya Angelou

In this chapter, we focus on how you can help your students synthesize claims and evidence to answer their compelling question, and help them represent this information in a creative way—visually and digitally. We also address digital and global literacies in support of creatively synthesizing information.

Our world is becoming more digital and more global. Literacy is not immune to these changes. Digital literacy and global learning are gaining interest as areas that our students will need in order to be full participants in our world. In 2015, Ron Ritchhart of Harvard asked a diverse group of teachers and school administrators: What do you want the children you teach to be like as adults? They wanted to see children grow up to be inquisitive, problem-solvers, empathetic, critical consumers, collaborative, adaptable, and citizens with a global perspective (Ritchhart, 2015). A major part of realizing this goal is to understand and embrace the possibilities technology offers (Johnson et al., 2016) to help develop well-adjusted and productive world citizens.

Students live in a world that is becoming more digitally and globally oriented and connected by the day (Alexander, Adams Becker, & Cummins, 2016; Alliance for Excellent Education, 2012). These connections are economic, environmental, political, social, and cultural. Students will need to acquire critical literacies in order to understand and interrogate global systems. Digital and global literacies are vital for middle and high school students to fully and productively participate in the world of tomorrow.

To embrace this modern reality, teachers and educational programs must also be digitally and globally connected. Students, meanwhile, need to experience this connectivity as relevant both to their own lives and to the world at large. They need to see the real-world application of what they are learning today and how it will help them succeed in whatever career they pursue in the future. However, if global connections are not enacted through a critical lens, considering inclusivity, equity, power, and privilege, they can do more harm than good.

CREATIVELY SYNTHESIZING INFORMATION

After students design their compelling question, and locate and analyze online sources, the next step is to creatively synthesize their information. The creative synthesis includes creating claims and evidence as well as representing the information in a visual way using digital tools.

Research has shown that students are challenged by synthesizing across sources (Coiro, 2011). In the past, English teachers taught the process of synthesizing across sources through a research paper notecard system. Students would write main ideas and key quotes from a source on notecards, one idea per notecard. Each idea should be related to the compelling question. If an idea is found not to be relevant to the compelling question, it should be set aside. This process would be repeated for each source. Then, the students would group like ideas together and label the group with the overarching or categorical theme. This process mimics an inductive, qualitative research approach used by social scientists and a literary analysis approach used by literary scholars. To bring this strategy into the 21st century, we have students use Haiku Deck or a similar tool. Each idea goes on one slide. Students can then drag and drop the slides to put like ideas beside one other.

Sometimes scientists and others use a deductive approach, where they begin with a hypothesis. For this type of inquiry, we have our students create an inquiry matrix (see Table 4.1). The columns are sources and the rows are proving or disproving the hypothesis. Each idea is placed in a separate cell corresponding to the appropriate row and column. Then students can look down the columns to see which columns have the most evidence and write their claim with multiple sources of evidence.

Table 4.1. Sample Inquiry Matrix

	Source 1	Source 2	Source 3	My Experiment
Evidence in Support of Hypothesis 1				
Evidence Disproving Hypothesis 1				
Evidence in Support of Hypothesis 2				
Evidence Disproving Hypothesis 2				

Conducting a creative synthesis as part of PBI is, in essence, a new creation. By this, we mean that when students synthesize information and represent it digitally, something new is created. You can model how to use concept maps, drawings, and diagrams to demonstrate mental connections between major concepts and details to help students synthesize information related to their compelling question. Digital templates, such as SmartArt graphics in PowerPoint, can help students determine the relationship between their ideas. For example, templates in PowerPoint include process, hierarchy, and cycle, giving students multiple choices and easing the cognitive load on students.

For an example, in one project, a 9th-grade student team collaborated to explore the compelling question: How does a lack of access to clean water and sanitation impact the physiological and emotional well-being of people? The team synthesized information from their annotated bibliography to create two claims with evidence to support their claims, as seen in Figure 4.1 on p. 58. Additionally, they created an infographic using the digital tool Piktochart (see Figure 4.2 on p. 59). The infographic represented their claims and evidence in a digital format to make their final project more appealing for a broad audience.

Reflect: How can you support your students to acquire the disciplinary skills of creating claims and supporting evidence during the inquiry process?

DIGITAL LITERACIES AND LEARNING

Given the large number of digital tools available for teachers, careful consideration is needed when deciding which tool to use in classroom instruction that supports students' disciplinary literacies and inquiry processes. To this end, the Technological Pedagogical and Content Knowledge (TPACK) framework (Mishra & Koehler, 2006) can help teachers make productive decisions about the best tools to use in their particular educational setting (see Figure 4.3 on p. 60). Based on Shulman's work (1986) on pedagogical content knowledge, Mishra and Koehler added technological knowledge, which resulted in a framework that has been researched extensively. TPACK is a reasoning process specifically designed to foster technology integration for educators. The framework describes how knowledge and technology, and pedagogy and content, interact when thinking about instruction. The TPACK framework is useful when deciding how to teach with technology and integrate it meaningfully into disciplinary instruction.

The following sections discuss digital approaches to gathering and locating information during an inquiry, as well as tools (such as web authoring and social networking) that can be used to design, showcase, and share the products of inquiry. We will also explore the affordances of using digital tools to design and develop your inquiry-based disciplinary literacy projects.

Figure 4.1. Student-Generated Claims and Evidence

ACCESS TO CLEAN WATER AND SANITATION CLAIMS SHEET

Claim 1

One of the world's greatest issues is inadequate sanitation and the lack of access to sterilized water, which has many negative effects on individuals worldwide. People need access to clean water because the lack of it can directly affect their health.

Evidence

According to the National Academy Press, worldwide over one billion people lack access to an adequate water supply (WHO/UNICEF, 2006). Unsafe water, poor sanitation, and the lack of hygiene account for an estimated 9.1% of the global burden of disease and 6.3% of all deaths, according to the World Health Organization (Prüss-Üstün et al., 2008). The need for access to clean water is not only seen in lower income countries but it is also seen in developing countries through water population and water shortages. If access to clean water and the necessary amount of sanitation is available to people globally, then the overall mental health and well-being will be vitally improved.

Claim 2

The access to immaculate water has strongly impacted the physiological well-being of the Sudanese people.

Evidence

Conflict and neglect have made water a scarce source. This is seen in the novel *A Long Walk to Water* by Nya's mom being extremely afraid when the family has to go to a big pond near Dinkas to get water during drought months. The consequence of having the pond as a water source resulted in internal conflicts between communities because of the limited access. Mothers and wives couldn't help but worry when sons and husbands left that they would run into a rival tribe. Thirty percent of South Sudanese people do not have access to clean water, which leads to disease (UNICEF). The limited access to water and sanitation has caused continually poor health status for everyone of all ages. People walk very long distances to have proper medical care. For example, Mawien Dut (Salva's father) has been in the clinic for stomach surgery—years of drinking dirty water have given him a nasty infection, but now he's ready to walk all the way back to his village (LitCharts). If the Sudanese people can acquire access to clean water, then there will be a decrease in emotional and physical distress within the country.

Used with permission from Christiana Akinyemi, Sydney Richmond, and Shania Williams.

Figure 4.2. Student-Created Infographic Using Piktochart

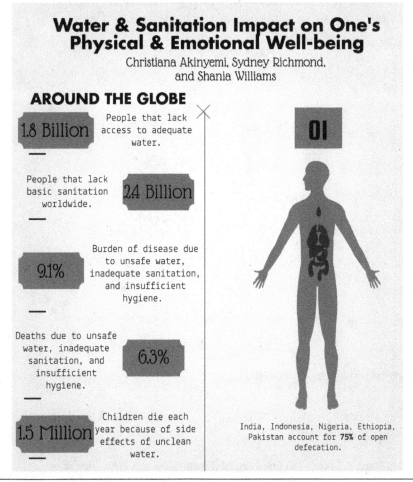

Used with permission from Christiana Akinyemi, Sydney Richmond, and Shania Williams.

Digital Tools

Teachers and students have many technology tools available to assist with gathering and analyzing information. These include social bookmarking and gathering tools such as Diigo, Evernote, LiveBinders, and Delicious. Free online tools like Weebly and Animoto allow teachers and students to easily design and showcase their inquiry projects. Popular social media platforms such as Twitter, Instagram, and Facebook provide dynamic venues where students can share their projects and receive immediate feedback from their

Figure 4.3. TPACK Diagram

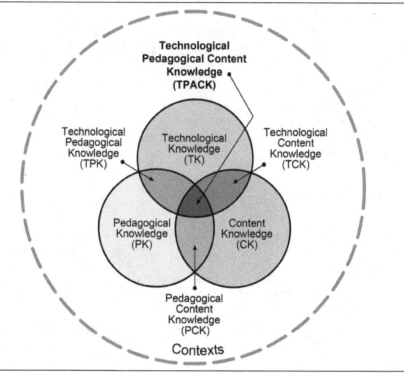

social networks, both locally and globally. Pinterest can help students gather and analyze information.

Using Digital Support to Enhance Multimodality and Transliteracies

Definitions of literacy continue to evolve to include student learning and creative processes that use multiple forms of communication and expression. The term *multiliteracies* was coined by the New London Group (1996) to describe an expanded approach to literacy that includes multimodal textual practices, such as linguistic, visual, audio, gestural, and spatial modes, as well as the assumption that literacies are culturally grounded. Jewitt and Kress (2003) defined *multimodal literacy* as the capacity to create meaning through many representational modes, often simultaneously. Arguments for literacy pedagogies that embrace visual and multimodal representation are well established in the academic literature (Bezemer & Kress, 2008; Kress, 2003; Ng, 2012). This suggests that multimodal texts offer students unique ways to both create and convey meaning (O'Brien & Scharber, 2008). In his discussion of multimodality and the capacity for transformation, Kress (2003) suggested that multimodal resources allow both content producers and consumers to reconfigure and redesign educational products to meet the specific needs of each user.

Teachers who embrace a transliteracies stance consider literacy as a social practice that fosters multimodal expression. Underscoring the ever-changing nature of literacy, language, and culture, transliteracies builds on the theoretical foundations of multiliteracies (New London Group, 1996) and New Literacy Studies (Street, 2003). Transliteracies marks a philosophical shift from the dichotomous perspective of print versus digital expression toward all literacies within a culture (Thomas et al., 2007). The *trans* prefix encourages teachers to bypass cultural or professional assumptions that privilege some literacies over others.

We discuss how students can incorporate digital tools into inquiry learning to actively explore and address the many complex challenges facing the world today while also reflexively examining their own beliefs and cultural perspectives. Using inquiry-based instruction, our particular pedagogical approach allows middle and high school students to investigate and problem-solve significant social issues at the local, national, and global levels.

Reflect: How can digital tools enhance the inquiry process in your classroom?

Critical Perspectives

Critical literacy approaches involve "reading, writing, speaking, listening, viewing, visually representing, inquiring, thinking, and acting from a critical frame" (Kerkhoff, 2017, p. 202). Freire famously said that critical literacy is to "read the word and the world" (Freire & Macedo, 1987, p. i). This means that students use literacy to question how power structures impact texts and everyday life. For example, readers question author bias and evaluate the credibility of claims based on whose voices are included and whose are left out. Writers construct claims by reading multiple sources to consider diverse viewpoints and to corroborate facts. Students apply critical literacy lenses to the world by examining power in society, breaking down oppressive systems, and building new social futures (New London Group, 1996).

Literacy has long been viewed as a component of citizenship and a social, cultural practice. What is new is applying the concepts to the world. For example, a common way to teach perspective-taking is to introduce students to the book *The True Story of the Three Little Pigs by A. Wolf*, a picture book written by Jon Scieszka and illustrated by Lane Smith. The book is written from the point of view of the Big Bad Wolf, who claims he was misunderstood. With global literacy, we would also talk about how misunderstandings can occur because of cultural differences or assumptions of culturally based norms, such as whether slurping one's food is considered a compliment or rude. We would take this lesson on perspective-taking a step further and show how newspapers in different countries report on the same event and discuss how our social, cultural, political, and historical perspective shapes how we view the world. In addition to these perspectives, Hull and Stornaiuolo (2010) suggest that global literacy involves an ethical dimension. They describe the ethical dimension as "cosmopolitan dispositions and habits of mind" (Hull & Stornaiuolo, 2010, p. 89), which leads to the theoretical framework of cosmopolitan literacy.

Reading about other people and places is an obvious way to help students learn about the world, but we know that books can also perpetuate stereotypes or appropriate cultures. Teaching English through a critical lens brings questions of bias, power, and privilege to the forefront. So that curriculum and instruction in classrooms does not perpetuate stereotypes or re-create social hierarchies, it is essential that teachers help students develop both critical and global literacy.

PBI GLOBAL AND EDUCATIONAL COSMOPOLITANISM

Global literacy can mean different things to different people. It can refer to the percentage of people in the world who are counted as literate or initiatives toward 100% literacy in the world, or it can be a synonym for global competence and global citizenship in literacy research. Global literacy means the ability to analyze texts and issues with a critical lens and global perspectives; awareness and respect for world languages and cultures; a view of literacy as a social, cultural, and political practice; and assuming an identity as a global citizen (Dwyer, 2016; Kerkhoff, 2017; Yoon, Yol, Haag, & Simpson, 2018). Global competence is not only possessing the knowledge, skills, and dispositions needed for global literacy but being able to do so well. Global citizenship is an identity that sees oneself as connected to and part of the global community. Teachers can present critical global literacy education in a way that helps students develop an identity as a global citizen and helps students dismantle hierarchies and work for a more just world.

According to the Asia Society and the Organization for Economic Co-operation and Development (OECD) (2018), global competence is critical for innovation across many professional fields. To foster this competence, students need to develop cross-cultural mindsets to address society's most pressing challenges. Able to extend beyond national borders, and not restricted by time or space, digitalization is a key means for teachers and students to establish global connections and embrace cosmopolitanism.

The term *cosmopolitan* is derived from the Greek word *kosmopolites*, meaning "citizen of the world." The philosopher Diogenes (4th century BCE) was the first to describe himself as a citizen of the cosmos rather than of a particular polity (Hansen, Burdick-Shepherd, Cammarano, & Obelleiro,

2009). Scholarship on the theory and application of cosmopolitanism has recently expanded in a variety of academic disciplines, including education (Hansen, 2008; Wahlström, 2014). As the first scholar to use the term *educational cosmopolitanism*, Hansen (2008) claims that the concept helps frame an action-oriented worldview in which people proactively create positive change in their own lives and the world at large. This theory argues against remaining a passive spectator or victim in the face of local and global change. Contrasting cosmopolitanism with globalization and modernity, Hansen (2008) asserts that participants can actively help shape their lives and identities rather than letting outside forces do it for them.

Our world is complex, fast-paced, and interconnected. Students in middle and high school must remain informed about trends and events far beyond their locality, or even their national boundaries. To thrive in the modern world as informed citizens, and later as productive workers, students must develop a broad international perspective. We have adapted our PBI Model to be used also in a global instructional context. PBI Global (Spires, Himes, Medlock Paul, & Kerkhoff, 2019) facilitates vibrant academic immersion in global themes and cross-cultural interactions that can stretch across the planet. In the process, students learn how to address large-scale, real-world problems while collaborating with students from different countries or cultures.

PBI Global creates a collaborative educational context where students learn with and from one another while addressing the most pressing societal challenges of our time. This learning approach both celebrates universal human experiences and facilitates understanding and valuing our cultural and personal differences.

Border-Crossing Discourses

Lee (2018) developed the concept of border-crossing discourse (BCD) from Gee's (2015) theory of Big "D" Discourse, and is a way to think about students interacting and collaborating online across time, space, and culture. Gee (2015) asserts that Big "D" Discourse is defined by the ways in which students behave, interact, read, write, and speak, based on the identities of particular groups. BCD exists within digital online social groups, where people from different cultures communicate around a particular topic.

PBI Global is an example of where students engage in BCD as they collaborate to address enduring global challenges. The focus on addressing an important issue such as climate change, global water, or refugees, for example, helps motivate diverse students to negotiate their understandings across cultural and linguistic differences. BCD provides a theoretical stance for exploring digital literacy practices in global contexts, especially as students engage in the United Nations Sustainable Development Goals within the PBI Global process.

United Nations Sustainable Development Goals

Engaging students in ongoing global issues of concern enables them to become partners in solving a variety of major international problems (OECD, 2018). As part of its global mission, the United Nations (UN) adopted 17 Sustainable Development Goals for all countries to work toward achieving by 2030. The goals target ending worldwide poverty, fighting societal inequalities, tackling climate change, and other serious international challenges (see Figure 4.4). Sustainable Development Goal 4: Quality Education calls on nations to ensure that learners are provided with knowledge and skills to promote sustainable development through education that promotes, among other aims, human rights, gender equality, the culture of peace and nonviolence, and global citizenship, as well as the appreciation of cultural diversity and of culture's contribution to sustainable development. The UN also underscores the role of educators in teaching their students about its mission and ensuring that students understand its relevance to education, future professional roles, and ongoing citizenry.

We like to ask these questions of students: What would happen if teachers and students around the world spent class time addressing the enduring challenges that the UN has identified? What if they focused their intellectual energy on understanding pressing issues such as the lack of safe drinking water in many regions of the world? Or the plight of migrants and refugees fleeing political turmoil and persecution? With an outward-looking perspective, we could foster a generation of young people possessing the passion

Figure 4.4. United Nations Sustainable Development Goals

From un.org/sustainabledevelopment. Used with permission. (The content of this publication has not been approved by the United Nations and does not reflect the views of the United Nations or its officials or member states.)

and expertise needed to solve complex, enduring social problems negatively impacting billions of citizens across the planet.

With its explicit design and processes, PBI Global encourages teachers and students across disciplines and grade levels to focus their educational efforts on meeting these ambitious UN goals. The intended educational outcome is a generation of students infused with a passion for major global concerns and the expertise needed to solve them.

Providing academic structure for students to learn to collaborate across time, space, and cultures can also help them develop educational cosmopolitanism. Encompassing Wahlström's (2014) four attributes—self-reflexivity, hospitality, intercultural dialogue, and transactions of perspectives—educational cosmopolitanism can guide later college, career, citizenship, and community choices and actions. PBI Global fosters such attributes in middle and high school students. Working interculturally, students engage in self-reflexivity as they encounter intersections and contradictions between their own culture and the culturally unfamiliar. Students must be hospitable as they create safe and respectful spaces for individuals from different cultures to fully participate in conversations (Spires, Kerkhoff, & Fortune, 2018). Working with fellow students from around the world creates ongoing opportunities for intercultural dialogue and sharing of perspectives as meanings are negotiated and new ideas are generated (Spires, Medlock Paul, Himes, & Yuan, 2018).

Reflect: What is the significance of introducing your students to the UN Sustainable Development Goals as part of the PBI process?

The Case of PBI Global Addressing Refugees and Migrants

To begin designing a PBI Global, teachers at each participating school should consider their own curriculum and academic standards, as well as a global issue of social significance that connects to their instruction. Let's consider the example of a high school in the southeastern United States that formed a partnership with a state-of-the-art high school in China. These schools forged a multiyear relationship through their mutual connections with a U.S. university. Working together, the two schools decided to conduct a PBI Global on the theme "A World on the Move: Refugees and Migrants."

Ms. Santoro, the 10th-grade teacher at the U.S. high school, and Mr. Ge, her counterpart at the Chinese high school, chose to align the PBI Global with their standards for research and argumentative writing. The UN's Sustainable Development Goal 16 of Peace, Justice, and Strong Institutions connected directly with the curriculum at both schools. The topic of refugees and migrants proved to be a compelling topic for the young people. They learned that there were 68.5 million forcibly displaced people worldwide.

Within that number, 24.4 million were refugees and 57% of refugees world-wide came from three countries: South Sudan, Afghanistan, and Syria.

We recommend launching a PBI Global with a common reading about the project's chosen global theme. A variety of text types and genres can serve this purpose, including digital and print news articles, short stories, novels, and autobiographies. To generate students' interest in the topic of refugees and migrants, Ms. Santoro and Mr. Ge selected the novel *In the Sea There Are Crocodiles* by Fabio Geda, a story based on true events about a young boy's 5-year journey from Afghanistan to Italy, where he finally managed to claim political asylum at age 15. Incorporating books like *In the Sea There Are Crocodiles* that feature adolescent characters from other cultures is one way to foster empathy and understanding across cultural divides.

This PBI Global culminated with the U.S. students traveling to China for a face-to-face work summit with their student counterparts. For 2 months before the trip, the 35 students—15 enrolled at the U.S. high school and 20 at the Chinese high school—collaborated to develop their inquiry projects around the agreed-upon theme. Divided into six international teams, the students in the United States and China used apps like WeChat and the web-based word processor Google Docs to communicate across time, space, and cultural differences. Major team activities included posing initial theme-based questions, conducting in-depth research, and developing their digital PBI Global products, all the while working together to overcome communication and cultural barriers. Obvious challenges centered around the 12-hour time difference between the two countries, as well as language differences. The Chinese students spoke English as a second language; the U.S. students did not speak Mandarin, but they learned some phrases as the project progressed.

Once in China, the students met their international partners in person for the first time. The teams immediately began putting the final touches on their research-based responses to the PBI Global questions. As Mr. Ge put it: "There is no substitute for human contact. When they come into this room together, you can feel those energies collide. And you feel a spark. I felt it. They're working with the same idea and concept. My job is to stand back and be proud."

The students had the daunting challenge of getting acquainted, finishing and reviewing their two required digital products, and finalizing their presentations before a global showcase on the third day. The first digital project was an infographic using the digital tool Piktochart, which represented visually the answer to their compelling question. The second digital product was a short public service announcement (PSA) in video format that made an appeal for viewers to understand and support refugees and migrants. (To view students' compelling questions and infographic and video products, go to pbiglobalstudentsummit.weebly.com/showcase-artifacts.html) The event was streamed by local media in China so parents in the United States could see their children present their work in real time.

Ms. Santoro later reflected on the PBI Global summit:

> The PBI Global Student Summit was a transformative and life-changing experience for students involved. Rarely does a teacher get to travel the world with her students and watch the effect that combined global travel and education can have. I was fortunate to have this experience with them and I will never be the same. I am reminded of the very important job we have as educators to design authentic learning experiences that make a difference.

Shi, one of the Chinese students, commented, "Before this project, I hardly understood what refugees were. From my research and from making the PSA, I further understand what this problem is and how it affects the countries around it." Claudia, one of the U.S. students, remarked, "Working on this project and traveling to China has really inspired me. I want to go to every country now. Not just to visit. I want to figure out how to change the world for the better." Her comment attests to the power of global collaboration and its potential to open a student's world up to new possibilities.

As a final step, PBI Global required students to take action related to the project theme. Students chose to organize and host a school dance at the Chinese high school to raise funds to donate to the UN Refugee Agency (UNHCR). "I fervently believe that this experience will help my students to continue to see how they can address complex problems by collaborating with others both locally and abroad," Ms. Santoro reflected. "I believe that young adolescents like the students involved in this trip will combine their passion, intelligence, and willingness to serve a global community to create innovative solutions that affect positive change on our world. As a teacher, I am reminded by this experience that with students like this—our world is in great hands."

Reflect: How can collaborating across time, space, and cultures change your students' perspectives about the world?

Disciplinary PBI Globals

This particular PBI Global involved the interdisciplinary topic of refugees and migrants. Teachers can also conduct global projects targeting specific disciplines. For examples, see Table 4.2.

Table 4.2. Global Compelling Questions Targeting Specific Disciplines

Discipline	Compelling Question	Text

Mathematics	How can reasoning with ratios and rates help solve real-world and mathematical problems?	Earth.google.com
		
		1. Students will review what we have already learned about rates, ratios, and unit rates.
		
		2. After we review, students will log on to earth.google.com.
		
		3. Students will choose the "I'm feeling lucky" button. This will assign them a completely random place in the world. Students can click the button up to five times until they find a place they want to explore. They should be using "street view" on Google Earth.
		
		4. After doing some research, students will answer the following questions about their chosen location:
		
		  a. What is the currency of this location? Research the conversion rate for $1. Calculate the conversion rate for $5, $25, $50, and $100.
		
		  b. What is the current population of this location? The U.S. Census estimates that in the next year, our country's population will grow by 2%. Write and evaluate an expression to represent this growth in the targeted location.
		
		  c. Use the ratio 1 meter = 3.281 feet to convert the area of this location in square feet into square meters.
		
		  d. What is the average temperature for this month at this location in Celsius and Fahrenheit?

ELA	How important is the maintenance and appreciation of beauty and art in times of horror?	Steven Galloway's *The Cellist of Sarajevo*

Table 4.2. Global Compelling Questions Targeting Specific Disciplines (continued)

Discipline	Compelling Question	Text
Science	How does the Amazon rain forest protect our environment? OR How do Kenyan cloud forests protect our environment?	*The Great Kapok Tree: A Tale of the Amazon Rain Forest* (drive.google.com/ open?id=13OAckqf-ZWsUG4DhhuD2TCR3 -R3eF3IP)
History/ Social Studies	What is the social model of disability? How does our school create barriers for different people? What can we do to support people with different needs?	Watch the documentary *Emmanuel's Gift* (about Emmanuel Ofosu Yeboah) This documentary tells about a young man (Emmanuel) born in Ghana. As a person with a disability in a country without established rights for those with disabilities, Emmanuel learned how to ride a bike and rode across the country promoting acceptance and support for people with disabilities. • Identify and chart: WHO participated, WHY did people protest, and WHAT changed because of this action? • Help students understand that the same issues arise all around the world—and each location is at a different point in the journey to equity—including right here!

Multiple Ways to Connect Globally

Obviously, not all teachers will be able to have their students travel to another country the way Ms. Santoro did. But there are many ways to collaborate globally with other classrooms. The easiest way for teachers and students to participate with global partners is to join an existing online project. Groups have already been created to provide support for collaboration, so there is a low bar for getting started (see Table 4.3.) For example, ePals has been around for over 20 years and provides several ways for you to connect with other teachers and classrooms from around the world. To get started, sign up for a free account. Then search (by age group, language, or country) for a class that will be a good match for your class based on your instructional goals. The site features collaboration projects, which can be joined by many teachers from around the world. The projects cover a variety of topics, some

Table 4.3. Digital Platforms for International Collaboration

Platform	URL	Discipline
ePals	epals.com/#/connections	Interdisciplinary
TakingITGlobal	tigweb.org	Interdisciplinary
Global Read Aloud	theglobalreadaloud.com	ELA, History/ social studies
Write the World	writetheworld.com	ELA
Write 4 Change	write4change.org	ELA
Mystery Skype	education.microsoft.com/skype-in-the-classroom/mystery-skype	Any discipline
iEARN-USA	us.iearn.org	Interdisciplinary
Students of the World	studentsoftheworld.info	Any discipline
International Literacy Day	literacyworldwide.org/ild	Any discipline
International Dot Day	thedotclub.org	Any discipline
Project Noah	projectnoah.org	Science

of which align with the UN Sustainable Goals. Connecting your classroom with students from another country has the potential for powerful learning experiences to happen. A resource like ePals not only builds student engagement but also broadens students' worldview.

Pernell Ripp (2017) advances the definition and advantages of authentic global collaboration by highlighting four key features:

1. Going beyond product-sharing, including give-and-take among collaborating groups
2. Creating products and processes with the intention of sharing with others
3. Targeting audiences mostly outside of school
4. Collaborating to add value to products, thus causing the inquiry learning process to change

Shared learning experiences in which students co-construct disciplinary knowledge and related products propels them to entertain new cultures as well as develop understanding for ways of living and being outside their own world.

SUMMARY

In this chapter, we focused on how you can help your students synthesize claims and evidence to answer their compelling question, and help them represent this information in a creative way—visually and digitally. Synthesizing claims and evidence is the core of disciplinary literacy for deeper learning, as this is when students are thinking critically about what they are reading and constructing logical arguments based on the evidence they have gathered. This phase is often the most challenging for students. In addition to critical thinking, students also use creative thinking in this phase. Students can use digital and global literacies in support of creatively synthesizing information. Critical and creative thinking are essential for literacy in the 21st century.

Now It's Your Turn!

Begin thinking about how your students will display their creative synthesis of claims and evidence through the thoughtful use of digital tools. Select at least one digital tool to introduce to your students during your PBI. Be sure to select a tool that supports the disciplinary literacy in which you want your students to engage. Tools we've used during PBI include these:

Animoto (animoto.com): online software that provides users with a variety of templates and drag-and-drop options to create professional videos for sharing

Canva (canva.com): allows users to access built-in photographs, graphics, and fonts for designing web and print media templates

Flipgrid (flipgrid.com): a video discussion platform; users can record, edit, and share videos and comment

Padlet (padlet.com): allows users to interactively post documents, texts, videos, and images to a project board for sharing and collaboration

Piktochart (piktochart.com): a web-based infographic application that allows users to create infographics and visuals using built-in templates

VoiceThread (voicethread.com): an online tool for teachers and students to create, share, and comment on a variety of media (including PowerPoint presentations and videos) using multiple inputs (including webcam and phone uploads)

Weebly (weebly.com): allows users without any coding experience to create websites using templates

Also, consider how you might include critical and global literacies within your PBI.

CHAPTER 5

Critical Evaluation as Summative and Formative Assessment

I am different. Not less.

—Temple Grandin

I explicitly inform students what successful impact looks like from the outset.

—John Hattie

We know that assessment is a critical aspect of teaching and learning. As you're moving through your PBI process, it's important to have assessments in place so you can critically evaluate how students are putting their reading and writing to work within the discipline. Having assessments throughout the PBI is essential for both deep content learning and high-quality student products.

One of the best opportunities to see how students can put their reading, writing, and language skills and strategies to work is to use them in the real world. Inquiry projects—where students examine a concept, analyze texts, synthesize that information, and then share the findings—allow teachers to assess literacy practices within an authentic context. Previous research has shown that assessing student skills in decontextualized ways can be biased against students who aren't well versed in academic language (Delpit, 2005).

In the PBI process, students are engaging in reading, writing, speaking, and listening en route to developing an authentic final product for an authentic audience. There are multiple opportunities, therefore, to assess disciplinary literacy as well as to assess disciplinary content knowledge and understanding of big ideas through both the process and the products. Additionally, providing ample time and space for multiple revisions empowers students and puts them on the path to creating successful, impactful products as a result of their inquiry. In this chapter, you will deepen your understanding of summative and formative assessment strategies and explore how to use strategies for differentiation as part of the PBI process.

SUMMATIVE ASSESSMENT

Though it may seem counterintuitive to begin with summative assessment, beginning with the end in mind helps align your design of the PBI process with your larger learning goals for students. When we approach learning with an inquiry stance, we aren't as concerned with coverage of curricular topics, but instead we think about the larger disciplinary concepts, also called enduring understandings and big ideas (Short, 2009; Tomlinson & McTighe, 2006).

Reflect: What concepts do *you* believe are the
most important for students to learn in your discipline?

In addition to conceptual knowledge, knowledge can be factual, procedural, and metacognitive (Anderson & Krathwohl, 2001). For example, in 6th-grade science, students study the topic of endangered frogs to understand the disciplinary concept of ecosystems; they learn that when one part of an ecosystem is disrupted, the whole ecosystem is disrupted. While studying this concept, students are also engaging in the scientific method, or a process by which scientists construct knowledge. In order to make sure that students are learning the key concepts and disciplinary processes connected to state and national standards, teachers need to assess student learning.

Our classrooms, much like the rain forests with the endangered frogs, are also an ecosystem. When a student falters on one part of the process or misunderstands one part of the project, the entire project is affected. If we wait until the end to determine how students will be assessed, it's too late for students who had missteps to correct course. That is why it is important for teachers to be clear and up front about the expectations and the learning goals for the project and to articulate the relationship of the learning goals with how students will be assessed (Hattie, 2008).

Rubrics

When you take on this kind of assessment—a process that involves using reading, writing, and language to help carry out inquiry projects in a discipline—there are a lot of challenges. One of the biggest challenges is the open-ended nature of project tasks, and how you assess whether or not students are on the desired trajectory. Teachers must decide what really matters and then ask themselves, "What counts as evidence that students are able to apply their disciplinary literacy skills to this inquiry project?" Based on the answer to this question, teachers create a rubric with a set of attributes or criteria that they're looking for, and use it to explicitly convey to students how they will be evaluated. The rubric guides assessment of whether or not the students (individually or sometimes as a group) are engaging in those tasks and exhibiting those kinds of knowledge, skills, and dispositions that mark excellence in the teacher's view (Tomlinson & McTighe, 2006). While factual knowledge is binary—either students know something or they don't—conceptual, procedural, and metacognitive knowledge and disposition are about degree. Rubrics allow teachers to assess the extent of a student's achievement along a continuum. A good rubric can be instructive, but a hastily constructed rubric can be detrimental to the learning process. It's important that the rubric be clear about what matters, yet not so prescriptive that students are writing to the rubric instead of writing for their audiences. Rubrics can be a tool for open-ended assessment like PBI, because they provide common standards without resorting to standardization.

Reflect: In PBI, what can count as evidence of literacy?

Because of the digital nature of the products, a well-developed rubric includes the intellectual and aesthetic qualities that are important to the discipline. In today's multimodal, highly visual communications world, students need to design both the message and the carrier of that message to reach a wide audience (Bishop & Counihan, 2018). To help students develop sophisticated digital products, it is helpful if you provide examples for the students to examine (such as infographics, videos, and Prezis) along with a sample rubric, and have the students work in groups to assess the products using the rubric. This provides the students with clear frameworks for what they are expected to create and what you as the teacher are looking for. A well-designed rubric also allows space for creative development on the part of the students while simultaneously meeting teacher expectations.

The rubric may be teacher-generated, student-generated, or a combination of the two. We have learned that a rubric jointly developed by teacher and students often helps students stay motivated during the project, since they have direct input into the learning goals; it also serves as guided instruction in what a high-quality product in that discipline looks like, because students have to consider and discuss the criteria and qualities that are important in the discipline.

Reflect: What makes a rubric helpful to learning?
What makes a rubric detrimental?

Three-Tiered Evaluation

To ensure broad-based and high-level feedback for their final products, we suggest that students engage in a three-tier evaluation process: self-evaluation, peer evaluation, and outside expert evaluation. Each tier of evaluation and revision is based on the same rubric. Self-evaluation gives students a chance to interact with the rubric and begin to develop a mental model of the quality required for their final products. Hattie and Zierer (2018) propose that feedback should involve three levels—task, process, and self-regulation—regardless of who is giving it. So, if students are self-evaluating their products, they should ask themselves: "What progress have I made on my goals and content?" (task); "What progress have I made on task completion?" (process); and "What progress have I made on self-regulation strategies?" (self-regulation).

Peer evaluation, from our experience, requires time and focused attention to be effective. Graham Nuthall (2007) found that the feedback peers provide often is not accurate, so teachers may tend not to value peer evaluation. We know, however, that peer evaluation can be helpful, but it is a skill that needs to be learned and practiced over time. For example, students may be afraid to point out problem areas that need development because they do not want to hurt a peer's feelings. Teacher modeling is essential to normalize the feedback process to help students develop the appropriate competence and mindset for peer feedback to be effective (Hattie & Zierer, 2018).

Outside expert evaluators (along with project coaches) are key to deep disciplinary learning and high-quality inquiry products. Finding volunteers to come into your classroom as outside experts can be challenging, but the benefits far outweigh the work of procurement. The value of that external feedback to students is the same value of writing for an external audience. To find external experts, start with your networks, and if that's not fruitful, reach out to your network's networks by asking your social media friends or teachers in a different school to share a request from you with their friends and family. External experts can come into the classroom face-to-face or virtually using Skype, Google Chat, or Zoom. We have been amazed at how willing experts are to share their knowledge and experiences with students. For example, when we were conducting a PBI on water, we asked an expert from the Water for South Sudan foundation to Zoom with a group of students to share firsthand the challenges of obtaining clean water, and what exactly was involved in successfully building a well in the region. The expert was more than willing to share her knowledge and was inspired by the work the students were doing.

We believe in the three-tier process for critically evaluating and revising, where students receive and are able to address feedback before sharing their product. Using multiple sources of feedback based on the evaluation rubric, students revise their products accordingly. Revision is a place where deeper learning can happen because students are challenged to dig a little deeper in their inquiry than they were inclined to the first time, or to think in a different way than they did originally.

Revising written products is important in every discipline, but experts have different foci. For example, a historian might detect inconsistencies in evidence and revise to strengthen the credibility of claims, while a mathematician might critically question logic and revise for precision. The external expert helps the group see what a disciplinary expert would focus on in the revision process. At the same time, project coaches can provide individualized feedback within a group, so that each student is revising a part of the project that the coach has assessed as needing more practice.

Reflect: Why are multiple levels of feedback
important for deep learning in your classroom?

FORMATIVE ASSESSMENT

Just as we do not want to wait until the end to determine how learning will be assessed, we do not want to wait until the end to see if students understand the concepts and procedures and are meeting state and national standards. Teachers can provide ongoing support through formative assessments, which should contain multiple sources of evidence of student learning rather than rest on one product, assessed one time. Tomlinson and McTighe (2006) refer to one-time assessment as a snapshot, and instead urge teachers to think of assessment as a photo album, containing evidence of learning from different angles and lenses evaluated at different times. Disciplinary literacy assessment, by nature, involves inferences by the teacher. We cannot see a student's content knowledge, reading comprehension, or conceptual understanding, so we collect information to make an evaluation of their knowledge, skills, and understanding. Having more than one source of information, a photo album, is more reliable than depending on one product, a snapshot.

Objective

The objective of formative assessment is to provide ongoing feedback that can be used by students to improve their learning, but the process can also be used by teachers to improve or clarify their instructional approaches. Often, teachers may not realize the benefit of formative assessment for their own professional growth as a teacher.

Formative assessment serves three purposes:

- It provides a photo album of evidence of students' learning.
- It guides the teacher's instruction because the teacher responds to what students need based on the assessment of their learning gaps.
- It enables the teacher to differentiate instruction to meet the different needs of students.

A formative assessment to capture students' understanding of the disciplinary concepts you are teaching does not need to be complicated. It can

Figure 5.1. Formative Assessment of Big Ideas Using Both Sides of an Index Card

Side 1	Side 2
Based on our study of _____, tell me a big idea that you understand. I understand . . .	Identify something about _____ that you do not yet fully understand. I do not **yet** fully understand . . .

be as simple as passing out index cards: Give each student one card. Display the instructions from Figure 5.1 on the board. It's important that students write the sentence stems so they learn to express their thoughts in complete sentences, the way experts do. The word *yet* is significant (Dweck, 2006), as it communicates to students that their understanding is not dependent on their aptitude but on their willingness to put in the time and effort needed to understand. You can have students complete these anonymously as a whole-class check, or you can ask them to put their name on the card to differentiate instruction the next day.

More examples of formative assessments can be found in Table 5.1. More information on differentiation will be provided later in this chapter.

As mentioned above, feedback is tied to learning. Going further, Hattie and Timperley (2007) demonstrated that when students receive feedback from teachers and peers in a way that is connected to *ongoing* learning, or what the researchers call a feedback loop, students showed a 29% gain in achievement—almost double the gain found for traditional interventions. As Grant Wiggins (1998) stated, "You can't learn without feedback. . . . It's not

Table 5.1. Examples of Formative and Summative Assessments by PBI Phases

Phase	Formative	Summative
Ask a Compelling Question	Share out with whole-class discussion as feedback	
Gather and Analyze Sources	Teacher observation checklist	Annotated bibliography
Creatively Synthesize Claims and Evidence	Graphic organizer	Claims sheet
Critically Evaluate and Revise	Self-, peer, and external expert review of final product using rubric	
Share, Publish, and Act	Exit-ticket reflection on what went well and what the student would change for the next PBI	Teacher grade of final product using rubric

teaching that causes learning. It's the attempts by the learner to perform that causes learning, dependent upon the quality of the feedback and opportunities to use it" (p. 46). John Hattie (2008), whose research has demonstrated that feedback has a substantial impact on student achievement, admitted that he has worked over time to understand exactly what helpful feedback involves. Teachers can divide the larger PBI into smaller assignments, with due dates leading up to the final due date, and provide feedback at each juncture.

Reflect: How can you design formative assessments
for your students during the PBI process?

Just-in-Time Instruction

When conducting PBI, teachers begin by helping students build the necessary background knowledge. But the teacher doesn't have to front-load all the instruction. Receiving all the information necessary to complete the project at one time can become cognitive overload for the students, meaning that they may not have the mental energy necessary to digest it all at once, or they may not have sufficient background knowledge to relate the learning to when and where they will need to apply it. Alternatively, teachers can provide just-in-time instruction throughout the inquiry process, either in anticipation of a sticking point for students or in response to a formative assessment.

During PBI, just-in-time instruction can be informal conversations with groups or formalized into a planned mini-lesson. Mini-lessons are short, usually 7–10 minutes, with embedded checks for understanding, such as "fist-to-five," where students show their level of understanding from zero (a fist) to full understanding (showing five fingers). In our experience, creating good compelling questions is difficult for students, so we normally plan for a mini-lesson before students begin that phase. After a fun and energizing PBI launch, we provide a mini-lesson on compelling questions. We begin with explicit instruction on what makes a question compelling: Is it open-ended (not a yes-or-no answer)? Does it result in an original product (not something that Google could answer)? Is it researchable (not impossible for the students to answer in the time allotted)? And is it something the students want to answer?

We then have students work in their PBI teams to create a compelling question. Each team is encouraged to write at least three questions related to their topic and of personal interest to the team members, and then to choose the best question to share with the whole class. The teams share their question and their rationale for why that question is compelling. The class then votes on whether or not the question is compelling, and classmates give feedback as to why or why not. Having a strong question is the foundation for a strong inquiry process. We find that by the end of this activity, students have a solid understanding about what makes a good research question, and each team has a solid compelling question to begin the PBI process.

Just-in-time learning also can be in response to formative assessment or teacher observation of misunderstandings or missteps. As students are working in groups, teachers can float around, asking content-knowledge questions as well as observing teamwork, problem solving, and students' contributions. Teachers can provide feedback and guidance to those individuals who need support; if a teacher notices a pattern of misunderstanding, the teacher can address the entire group or class.

Just-in-time instruction and formative assessments are integral to the PBI process. Formative assessment can be self- or teacher-evaluated and can be informal checks for understanding or more formal assignments with due dates. An example of an informal self-assessment is fist-to-five, while examples of teacher-evaluated formative assessments are collecting 1-minute essays, journal entries, and exit slips. Teachers use assessment not only to evaluate, but also to provide feedback and differentiation on students' content knowledge to help the students achieve deeper learning.

In all, the purpose of assessments is to inform teaching and learning. As students are conducting their inquiry projects, assessments allow teachers to differentiate instruction by revealing the gaps in students' understandings or skills. By combining the ideas of formative and summative assessment, the teacher is using a powerful pedagogical approach that allows students to enter an iterative design process with important feedback along the way.

Reflect: How are formative assessments related to differentiated instruction?

DIFFERENTIATION

Differentiation means that we are very clear about learning outcomes but flexible about the way students reach these goals (Tomlinson, 2017). In other words, we hold high expectations for all students, but we provide different paths to learning. Relating disciplinary literacy and differentiation means that we provide a variety of ways for students to access and practice disciplinary literacy. It does not mean that readers labeled as struggling are given basic literacy instruction while those labeled as advanced are given disciplinary literacy instruction. Research has shown that all students, including those labeled as struggling, benefit from a disciplinary literacy lens, and it should not be reserved for "advanced" readers (Learned, 2018). We can differentiate by learners' readiness in a way that meets learners where they are without watering down the curriculum, and we can differentiate by interest to be responsive of their personalities, curiosities, passions, and goals.

Differentiation in Each Phase of the PBI Process

The most obvious way to differentiate the Ask a Compelling Question phase is to allow students to follow their own interest and curiosity about the curriculum topic under study. Groups of differing ability levels and areas of talent can thus be determined based on interests. This provides an authentic way to form heterogeneous groups. Interest is an important form of differentiation, but not the only form. Teachers can also differentiate based on student readiness. For students who are not ready to write their own compelling questions, teachers can provide question stems such as those shown in Table 5.2. Providing students with the language to frame their idea helps alleviate the cognitive burden of language formation. The question stems also guide students toward open-ended questions rather than yes-or-no questions. Using the stems can help students generate several questions and then they can choose the best one.

The Gather and Analyze Sources phase can be differentiated by texts, process, and products (Tomlinson, 2017). The texts that are gathered can be differentiated by mode, such as videos, podcasts, journalistic articles, and research articles. Mode does not equal complexity, meaning that a video can provide just as much complex information on the students' question as a research article. Teachers can encourage students to collect multiple modes and not limit students to print-based lexicographic sources. The texts can

Table 5.2. Question Stems as a Scaffold for Generating Compelling Questions

Which? (Collect information to make an informed choice.)	Which . . . was the most effective at . . . ? Which was the most influential catalyst for . . . ?
How? (Understand problems and perspectives, weigh options, and propose solutions.)	How does hindsight help us understand . . . ? How did . . . get this way? How would . . . solve . . . ? How does . . . impact . . . ? How has . . . changed over the period of . . . and why? How has . . . played a role in the evolution of . . . ? How will the use of . . . affect . . . ?
Why? (Understand and explain relationships to get to the essence of a complicated issue.)	Why does . . . ? Why did . . . behave/respond as they did during . . . ?
What if? (Use the knowledge you have to pose a hypothesis and consider options.)	What does the research suggest will happen if . . . ? What can we learn from . . . ? What approaches might . . . ?

also be differentiated by reading level. Although we would never suggest that a learner should be limited to texts within a level provided by a standardized reading assessment, such assessments can be one helpful way to match readers and texts. Rewordify is an online tool that allows texts to be modified to make them easier to read. Newsela is a great resource for differentiating informational texts by students' Lexile level, which can often be found on state-mandated tests. But remember our warning about using one piece of evidence to assess students' abilities and knowledge: Lexile levels can be a good starting place, but teachers should also use their professional judgment to increase the text complexity of a student's reading assignments if the student has shown growth or has exceptional background knowledge on the topic.

Reflect: How can you match texts to readers during PBI?

The process for gathering sources can be differentiated through the amount of curation from the teacher. The teacher can curate all of the sources for students, providing students with a cart of relevant library books and a digital document with hyperlinked sources. Or students could be required to search for all their own sources. Or you can try a combination, having students do some of the library research and Internet searches and having the teacher provide a set number of required sources from a list of choices. This is a great opportunity to differentiate by learner needs. Some learners may need more scaffolding than others; teachers can provide sources for those who need the extra help, while other students will hone their searching skills by finding their own texts. In our experience, giving students choice in what they read helps increase motivation (Spires, Himes, Medlock Paul, & Kerkhoff, 2019). In addition, the Gather and Analyze Sources phase also can be differentiated by learning products. Groups can produce a list of sources, a bibliography created in the web-based application Citation Machine, or an annotated bibliography in proper Modern Language Association (MLA) format. The number of sources required can also be differentiated by readiness.

Creatively Synthesize Claims and Evidence can be a challenging phase for many students. For this phase, as with the others, differentiation can happen across groups and within groups. This phase can be differentiated by the amount of time spent modeling and practicing with students before they construct their own claims without teacher guidance. Some students may need to see constructing a claim modeled only once before they feel ready to begin constructing claims on their own and teaching the rest of their group along the way. Other groups may need to see multiple examples or have a chance to talk through the process and ask the teacher questions.

Using self-assessment can be a way to manage differentiation within groups during this phase. After a mini-lesson to the whole class on constructing claims, the teacher can ask the students to write a color that corresponds to their current level of understanding: green for *good to go*, yellow for *kind of understand*, and red for *need more help*. Those who marked green can go to work on their projects. Then the teacher can call the yellows and reds together and invite them to ask questions. The yellows may have questions already formulated. With the teacher, the yellows and reds can work through any gaps in knowledge or misunderstandings. Once a student understands, they are free to leave the discussion and join their group to work on their projects.

After the Creatively Synthesize Claims and Evidence phase, students critically evaluate and revise evidence as they fine-tune their claims within a discipline. A strategy that Leigh Hall (2014) recommends to help students who do not seem motivated to engage in reading and writing is to have students set their own disciplinary literacy goals. Because each student has different goals from the other students, the evaluation of whether the student has met the goals is personalized to the learner. As students work through the PBI process, it's important for the teacher to point out to each student the parts of the project that align to his or her disciplinary literacy goals. This can motivate the students to engage in those reading and writing activities because they see the connection to what is important to them.

Evaluating and revising doesn't have to wait until the end of the project. Using formative assessments throughout the process ensures that no group gets too far behind or too far away from the learning goals. By chunking the larger project into smaller assignments, students turn in parts of the project along the way, receive critical evaluation from the teacher, and then are able to revise based on individualized feedback before turning in the final project.

Supporting Students Labeled as
Special Education and English Language Learners

Accommodations and modifications are not the exact same thing as differentiated instruction (Tomlinson, 2017), but they are equally important. When there are students with Individualized Education Plans (IEPs) or labeled as English language learners (ELLs), advanced planning can help ensure that their needs are met. By explicitly teaching disciplinary literacy, teachers are following best practices for working with ELLs (Zygouris-Coe, 2012) and students with IEPs (Archer, 2011) by making the invisible visible. Using the explicit instruction model means being up front and clear about what students are to learn. Teachers are clear about the learning goals, the means to the goals, and providing the support needed for each student as long as it is needed (Tomlinson, 2017).

One way we ensure support for students with special needs is to bring in the students' case managers as project coaches. Each small group has a project coach who stays with them from the beginning of the project until the end. Because every group has a coach, no group is singled out. However, having a coach who understands how to modify assignments and accommodate based on students' individual circumstances ensures that each student's special needs are met.

For ELL students, it's important to facilitate collaborative classroom activities that support the development of student autonomy (Walqui & Lier, 2010). Essentially, teachers provide their students with opportunities that transcend the hierarchical "expert–novice" relationships that often transpire within an L1–L2 ELA classroom by providing students with language development opportunities that honor their home language and fall on all points of the conversational-academic language continuum. In doing so, teachers maintain high expectations for academic rigor while engaging students in focused conversations about curriculum based on students' lived experiences and interests.

For example, a teacher with the goal of helping students understand character development may choose to focus on the concept of freedom, a central theme in the anchor text, as her students have spoken about feeling free on the weekends or during summer break. The teacher does not present herself as an expert on freedom; rather, she engages students by starting the lesson with a writing task: "What does the word *freedom* mean to you? Where/how have you seen this word being used? Tell me about a time when you felt free." Language learners write their responses and are then given structured opportunities to share. After sharing their products with the class, students will have had opportunities to negotiate imaginative scenarios both conversationally and using the academic target language; they are working collaboratively to develop autonomy.

Another strategy for ELLs is to use groups of multimodal texts connected to the compelling questions (Heritage, Walqui, & Linquianti, 2016). Because no two students are alike, the development of disciplinary literacy in English will evolve at differing rates. The more you can teach conceptual inquiry lessons for the whole class, including ELLs, the more likely they will be able to learn from one another.

As the teacher implements a PBI, it's important to use time-honored strategies for ELLs to support their reading, writing, and thinking with disciplinary texts (Boley, 1985). Goldenberg (2008) suggests the following strategies specific to ELLs:

- Reviewing new vocabulary or concepts prior to the lesson, or spending additional time on these concepts during the lesson
- Making extended explanations; focusing on pictures, gestures, and other visuals
- Choosing familiar texts or texts that are similar to previous readings
- Having the teacher, student, or other students paraphrase or summarize materials after reading

- Allowing additional time for reading and writing activities
- Extending linguistic interaction with peers and teachers
- Using knowledge of the student's primary language as much as possible (p. 60)

Building these types of strategies into the PBI process for students, especially ELLs, will enable the students to have a deeper and richer learning experience as they conduct inquiry related to specific disciplines.

SUMMARY

This chapter aligns with the Critically Evaluate and Revise phase of PBI. After synthesizing claims, students critically evaluate and revise evidence as they fine-tune their claims within a discipline. A PBI that includes both formative assessments and differentiated instruction along with summative assessments means that students benefit by having their needs anticipated and receiving built-in supports to help them achieve deep disciplinary learning. The challenge with this type of assessment is that it is labor intensive. You have to use rubrics, and you have to apply them to each process and product that the students have created along the way, and provide multiple opportunities for revision. This process takes a lot of time and requires expert judgment from the teacher. Nonetheless, PBI is a great opportunity to see reading, writing, and language at work. Ultimately, the ability to use literacy to solve everyday problems is what it means for students to be college-, career-, and citizenship-ready.

Now It's Your Turn

Now you will design a rubric and a three-tiered evaluation for your PBI. By using the same rubric during formative and summative assessment, you are using a powerful pedagogical approach that allows students to enter an iterative design process with important feedback along the way.

Design the Rubric

Answer the following questions to guide your design of the rubric:

1. What are the disciplinary concepts you want students to know and understand as a result of this PBI?
2. What are the disciplinary literacy skills that you want students to be able to have as a result of this PBI?

3. What will count as evidence of having learned these concepts?
4. Will the criteria on the rubric be teacher-generated or teacher- and student-generated?

Design a rubric that targets the learning outcomes of your PBI. One of our favorite tools for creating rubrics is RubiStar (rubistar.4teachers.org/index.php). If you can, consult your students to help you generate the content of the rubric. If that's not possible, go ahead and design the rubric now and let them give you input at a later date. Make sure to finalize the rubric at the beginning of the PBI, and provide copies to students, coaches, and external experts.

Design the Three-Tier Evaluation

Answer these questions to guide your design of the three-tier evaluation:

1. How will you structure self-evaluation?
2. How will you structure peer evaluation?
3. Who do you know in the field related to your PBI topic who could serve as an external expert? If you don't know anyone, who do you know who might know someone? Or which social media networks could you engage with to find experts?

Reach out to external experts and ask them about providing feedback to your students. Make sure you really sell it! You can adapt or adopt the following wording in your message:

Dear [name], My class is doing exciting work in our [insert discipline] class this semester. In [month], we will be researching [topic], and I could really use your help! Since you are an expert in the field, my students would really benefit from hearing from you. To participate, you would look at each of the group's projects and give them feedback. This can be done face-to-face or virtually through Skype during our class from [give time range]. It would probably take 1 hour on each of 2 days for you to talk with each group. Are you interested? Do you know of anyone else who may be interested?

It's good to get additional names from your contacts in case something falls through with the expert you've lined up.

CHAPTER 6

Share, Publish, and Act
Students and Teachers Stepping into Leadership

The great aim of education is not knowledge, but action.

—Herbert Spencer

Be the change that you wish to see in the world.

—Mahatma Gandhi

In our final chapter, we explore how students can present their PBI findings and products of learning to a wide, authentic audience, and how they can act on their new knowledge—how they can Share, Publish, and Act. Additionally, we conceptualize this final PBI phase as a teacher leader process, and discuss how teachers can continue their disciplinary literacy journey beyond the classroom.

STUDENTS SHARE, PUBLISH, AND ACT AS PART OF THEIR PBI PROCESS

Nothing is more motivational than an authentic audience to inspire students to share and celebrate their accomplishments from the PBI process. Whether the audience is live or virtual, students need an outlet to encourage them to put their best foot forward and to reflect deeply on their experience.

Publishing their PBI products on social media is an easy way to reach a global audience: Students can design an entire social media campaign and publish on multiple platforms, developing their activist and leadership abilities as they reach a worldwide audience. When students construct knowledge, create representations of that knowledge, and communicate to an authentic audience, they are no longer imitating experts in a discipline; they are becoming part of the disciplinary community (Wilder & Msseemmaa, 2019).

In addition to a virtual global audience, students can share their PBI products and process with a "real-life" audience via a showcase that bridges the PBI experience with students' schools, homes, and communities.

Celebrating success is an important part of the disciplinary process; inviting families, administrators, other students, and community members to the showcase provides an authentic local audience and a celebratory atmosphere. Making their work public motivates students to do their best work and invites the community to engage with students on what they are learning at school. Students share what they have learned about the disciplinary topic under investigation, and also the process they undertook as members of the disciplinary community—what they learned about inquiry, problem solving, collaboration, communication, and activism. As John Dewey (1933) famously said, "We do not learn from experience . . . we learn from reflecting on experience" (p. 78).

The "act" part of Share, Publish, and Act involves students acting on their new knowledge with activities such as community service projects. While serving the community, teachers and students can advocate for needed improvements or social change as they forge creative spaces that support communities to also engage in the learning process.

Reflect: How can you design a PBI showcase that supports students to Share, Publish, and Act on what they have created through disciplinary literacy?

TEACHER LEADERS AS CHANGE AGENTS

Teachers are assuming more leadership roles at both the instructional and organizational levels of practice, and the concept and practice of teacher leadership continues to gain momentum. As Robyn Jackson, an author for the Association for Supervision and Curriculum Development (ASCD), noted:

> We [need to] have teachers strategically placed so that they are able to step inside the practice of other teachers and help expand [those teachers' practices] and then [those other teachers] become better. . . . The definition [of teacher leader] transcends formally defined roles in the building. With that definition, every teacher, any teacher, at some point in their career, becomes a teacher leader. (ASCD, 2015, p. 8)

Some roles are formal, with a designated title and responsibilities, while other roles are more dynamic and fluid as teachers construct new identities—as they interact with their peers and become problem-finders as well as problem-solvers within the school context. In a review on teacher leadership, York-Barr and Duke (2004) synthesized the many acts that teacher leaders are involved in, from mentoring other teachers to working with peers, bringing about school change, presenting at and leading professional organizations, and becoming politically active to support education.

Teacher leaders contribute to the overall school culture, impact learning for all students, and influence instructional practices of peers. In short, teacher leaders are critical to a high-functioning school and learning environment. As you begin your journey as a teacher leader in disciplinary literacy, we offer several simple suggestions for how you can get started, adapting comments from José Vilson, a middle school math teacher from New York who blogs for Edutopia (Vilson, 2013; quotation marks indicate direct quotes from Vilson):

> First, "know your stuff." Learn as much as you can about disciplinary literacy and how to apply it. Obviously, you are an expert in your discipline, but you can also provide resources and support for teachers of other disciplines as they apply new strategies in the classroom and acquire new dispositions about their responsibilities as a literacy teacher.
>
> Second, "create something new." Spend time thinking about how to create new practices and ways for working with disciplinary literacy. Adapt what you learn from others to support your colleagues. If you have not been presenting at conferences, take the next step by talking to your principal or applying for grant funds to share your professional ideas on disciplinary literacy.
>
> Third, "structure your role." Make sure you and your administration are clear about your role as a teacher leader within your school. If there is ambiguity, you may become frustrated because of conflicting goals within your organization. As your school makes changes around disciplinary literacy practices, identify what you do best and start making things happen. It's easy to overextend yourself, so spend time and energy enlisting other key teachers to help make changes at your school.
>
> Fourth, "keep the energy going." The biggest lesson we have learned as educators is to stay on course when trying to implement new ideas. Don't give up if things don't run smoothly at first, and don't give up if things start off well and then become bumpy. Find creative ways to keep your colleagues energized and excited about disciplinary literacy practices.

Lieberman and Friedrich (2010) discuss the context in which teachers implement change by explaining that it is a combination of (1) accountability for student achievement through standardized testing, and (2) creating a coherent vision of teaching and learning across the school system, taking diversity into account. In most schools, both of these approaches are in play and often create organizational tensions in the absence of strong leadership at the school and district level. Teachers have the daunting task of navigating their way through these tensions.

Reflect: How do you envision being a change agent
in your classroom, your school, and beyond?

Teacher Leadership at the Classroom Level

Supporting students as they Share, Publish, and Act requires leadership. The keys to good leadership outside the classroom apply in the classroom as well, and include goal-setting, communication, and motivation. As the leader in the classroom, you will be providing the vision for the project by setting expectations for what a high-quality process and product looks like in your discipline.

Students working in groups of peers also present opportunities for teachers to develop student leadership. Teachers can be explicit with group leaders about the expectations for the day and allow them to figure out how to get their group to accomplish their tasks and goals. This technique works especially well for groups in which one person takes it upon her- or himself to complete the work. The teacher can communicate to this student that the expectation is for *all* group members to contribute to the inquiry product. This shifts the focus of the student completing the work for the group to supporting the student in leading the group. Rather than telling the group leader how to motivate or to delegate, give the leader the opportunity to problem-solve.

Teacher Leadership at the School Level

Teacher leaders adopt "inquiry as stance" (Cochran-Smith, & Lytle, 2009; Lytle, Lytle, Johanek, & Rho, 2018) to teaching and learning, organizing professional learning communities (PLCs) where collaborative inquiry rather than transmission through PowerPoint is the professional development model (Skerrett, Warrington, & Williamson, 2018). As a community, teachers ask questions, dialogue, share what works, and reflect on learning. Some schools have formalized and institutionalized professional learning communities as part of the school's plan, but PLCs can also be informal groups of colleagues who choose to support one another's professional growth.

When teacher communities take an inquiry stance to learning, a shared responsibility for learning is embedded and dispersed throughout the community (McConachie & Apodaca, 2010). A teacher leader can initiate disciplinary literacy as a broad topic that teachers can investigate to improve students' reading, writing, and thinking. The teacher leader can initiate conversations for establishing shared goals and co-created norms. Gallimore, Ermeling, Saunders, and Goldenberg (2009) found that using school-based inquiry teams to solve instructional problems significantly improved student achievement. The inquiry process shifted attribution of student achievement to teachers' actions rather than external causes. As a result, teachers began to buy into the adage "You haven't taught until they've learned" (p. 551).

Charner-Laird, Ippolito, and Dobbs (2016) found that inquiry-focused PLCs within disciplines benefited from a teacher leader who provided structure to meetings and synthesized the many voices to create meaning aligned with the group's goals. The teacher leader's facilitation was essential to the success of the inquiry process and to participants' professional growth. If you feel that you do not have enough experience with disciplinary literacy yet to lead professional learning communities, think again! The study found that teachers "liked working with a leader who was also learning how to enact disciplinary literacy alongside them" (p. 989). Interdisciplinary grade-level teams can purposefully use the same literacy strategies, with the goal of horizontally aligning literacy skills and academic language to create consistency for students among different disciplines.

Whether PLCs are within or across disciplines, conflict can arise. As a teacher leader, how you guide the conflict can determine whether the PLC becomes a fruitful place of growth or a place of frustration. Productive conflict can play an important role in helping PLCs matur and become more effective in helping teachers grow (Lieberman & Friedrich, 2010). PLCs are often the place "where the uncertainties and questions intrinsic to practice can be seen (not hidden) and can function as grist for new insights and new ways to theorize practice" (Cochran-Smith & Lytle, 2009, p. 37). As teachers develop enough trust to share their ideas about teaching and learning, as well as to share their vulnerabilities, members of the PLC form a stronger bond. Additionally, when student achievement improves in direct response to the content and process of the PLC collaboration, teachers become more empowered and develop a greater sense of professional satisfaction.

Figure 6.1 is a sample agenda for how to lead a PLC session on using close reading for disciplinary literacy. Note that you as a teacher leader are required to provide structure for the session by leading your colleagues in modeling a close reading, developing a video of yourself conducting a close reading, and then reflecting on how you will use close-reading activities to encourage disciplinary literacy in your own classes.

Teacher Leadership at the State, National, and International Levels

Teacher leaders can become involved in state- and national-level professional organizations. The most direct way to become involved is to submit a proposal to present at a conference. Many of the teachers we have worked with have paired with a colleague to co-present at conferences; when getting started, this lessens the pressure. Examples of discipline-based national organizations include the following:

- National Council of Teachers of English: ncte.org
- National Council for Social Studies: socialstudies.org
- National Science Teachers Association: nsta.org
- National Council of Teachers of Mathematics: nctm.org

Figure 6.1. Sample Agenda for How to Lead a PLC Session on Disciplinary Literacy

The purpose of this facilitation guide is to support your professional learning community (PLC) sessions. The guide is intended to help you lead a 60-minute PLC session on how to conduct a close reading as part of a PBI project.

I. TEACHER TALK: MODELING A CLOSE READING (25 minutes)

This strategy can be used with many different texts. When choosing your text, make sure it is rich, dense, and complex. Steps for your next activity:

a. Bring a dense text that your students will read. Some examples include:

ELA: a literary criticism of a poem or an informational text used to expand some concept the author uses

Science: part of their textbook with graphs and charts and rich explanatory paragraphs

History/Social Studies: part of their textbook with numerous terms, concepts, and ideas from economics

Mathematics: an introduction to new math concepts in the textbook

b. Organize and script your close reading.

c. As you read and annotate, deliberately apply literacy strategies: What is the author saying? (author's purpose and how the text is organized); Are there any hard or important words? (think Tier 2 and Tier 3 vocabulary); What does the author want me to understand? (apply needed prior knowledge and making connections to other physical aspects of the text—that is, headings, bold words, graphs, charts, footnotes). How does the author play with language to add to meaning? (look at sentence structure and length, confusing sentences, and the accompanying diction).

d. Apply deliberate disciplinary strategies to your close-reading script.

ELA: Differentiate speaker from author's point of view; analyze author's voice and style; identify literary and rhetorical devices and author's purpose in using them; construct claims; make personal, intertextual and global connections to information.

Science: Explain how you determine abstract concepts; generate hypotheses with the content; analyze cause-and-effect patterns; synthesize the dense information; reflect on the author's bias and your own.

History/Social Studies: Focus on author, purpose, and audience; infer to make initial suggestions and claims; compare source information with prior knowledge and reconcile any tension; begin making arguments for or against information.

Mathematics: Read and interpret symbolic notations, graphic representations; analyze logic of argument; understand mathematical terms/concepts; apply prior knowledge to new information.

(continued on next page)

Figure 6.1. Sample Agenda for How to Lead a PLC Session on Disciplinary Literacy (continued)

e. Share your annotations with a colleague in your discipline and give each other feedback on the quality of the annotations.

II. THEORY INTO CLASSROOM PRACTICES (25 minutes)

An effective lesson plan includes teacher modeling, guided practice, and independent practice. Your purpose for creating this activity is to deliberately guide your students through reading a dense text. Ultimately, in future student-centered lessons, students would apply these strategies as they read. Use this time to create a video of your close reading. The close reading is an integral part of the Gather and Analyze Sources phase of the PBI process. If you have time, students can then make videos of their own close readings and share in class.

III. REFLECTION AND WRAP-UP (10 minutes)

You have reflected on and modeled your own reading. You have applied your understanding of reading (in your discipline) to create a close reading of a dense text. Share with your colleagues how you will use close reading activities to encourage disciplinary literacy.

Another aspect of state and national leadership is being aware of current issues related to your discipline and advocating for your students and your profession. For example, a key issue in ELA is *translanguaging*—going beyond code-switching to allow hybrid language and to allow dialects in tested writing. Teachers of history and social studies have noted how the curriculum continues to be squeezed, and how, in one state, legislators are pushing for a class in finance literacy, which would reduce the number of history courses in high school. Using a disciplinary literacy lens, more time could be spent reading texts related to history and social studies during English language arts time. In science, teachers contend with climate change deniers as they teach their students to be science-literate. In mathematics, there is a push for more time for mathematical discourse (discussions) during class, and for teachers to share metacognition/metaknowledge of how mathematicians think to teach students how to communicate their thought processes during mathematical problem solving. Across all disciplines, teachers face excessive testing. Rachel, a middle school mathematics teacher we have worked with, stated, "It would be nice to have the time to dig into something and really get kids excited about coming up with and solving problems. Right now, we are just doing a bunch of [test] practice, and that's unfortunate" (Graham, Kerkhoff, & Spires, 2017, p. 78).

Additionally, teachers can leverage their online networks to collaborate and lead as part of a wider community of educators. For example, TeachersConnect provides an online forum in which teachers can collaborate and grow. A global movement, like #TeachSDGs, may also provide opportunities for teacher leadership through project development and online publication. TakingITGlobal and the Global Read Aloud are welcoming online communities of practice that situate the teacher within a global audience.

Teacher's Voices on Teacher Leadership with Disciplinary Literacy

As mentioned, teacher leaders can evolve in a variety of ways. Figures 6.2, 6.3, and 6.4 provide personal reflections on leading disciplinary literacy from three teacher leaders.

Teacher leaders spend time learning, observing, listening, and empathizing. Then they take their knowledge and experiences and *intentionally* take action to make a positive difference in the lives of students, teachers, parents, and other leaders.

We believe a school community thrives and experiences the most success when a distributive leadership model is in place—when each person on

Figure 6.2. Reflection of a Science Teacher Leader

Micki Powell, Science Teacher
Person County Early College High School for Innovation and Leadership
Roxboro, NC

To be a good leader, especially in the classroom and within your school, you need three characteristics: (1) the ability to see the needs and find ways you can fill them; (2) the ability to find good staff within your school to learn from; and (3) the true desire to see students learn and grow regardless of any measurable data. One thing you cannot control is your administration, but I have been blessed with administrators who were willing to let me be innovative.

Literacy is the key for any student to grow. Finding ways to incorporate literacy is crucial. Working with my team to find others who have used the PBI process with disciplinary literacy and begin to model what they were doing allowed us to adapt to our students' needs. As a science teacher, finding a novel that can be the basis for the cross-curricular nature of PBI was important. Being able to tie the story into a real-world context was imperative. My English, Spanish, and social studies teachers were the ones I relied on to promote that context to our project. My math teacher and I provided the data analysis components so students could experience that aspect of research. Being able to delegate when you are conducting a big project, like PBI, is what keeps you sane.

My best advice for being a teacher leader when conducting a schoolwide PBI is to select a diverse group of teachers from different disciplines and with different types of expertise so that you can truly collaborate. Keep an open mind—as a leader you should drive the collaboration but not the collaborators. Use their strengths to create something unique for your students to experience. Lastly, adapt or learn from people who have done what you want to do then make it what is best for your students.

Used with permission from Micki Powell

Figure 6.3. Reflection of a Mathematics Teacher Leader

Sharon Wright, Mathematics Teacher
Frontier Junior/Senior High School
Chalmers, IN

To be a good leader, you have to take initiative and then follow through with what you start. Teacher leaders create high expectations for their students and then inspire them to reach those expectations. When working with other teachers, a leader states a vision and then does what needs to be done to help others accomplish the vision.

For example, when enacting PBI with my grade-level team, I set the vision of working with the common topic of global hunger. Then, I encouraged each teacher to use the tools of their discipline to help the students learn more about the topic and meet the standards for their course. Throughout the process, I supported students in staying the course of the five phases of inquiry and I supported the other teachers in bringing their strengths (both disciplinary and personality) to the PBI.

I'm a mathematics teacher. Literacy isn't what I consider my strength, but I relied on the strengths of my co-teachers to make sure all of the literacy elements were in place so that students could solve the problem of their inquiry. And, I found when working with my co-teachers that I was able to support students in verbalizing their problem solving because that is something we work on in mathematics class. So, while I wouldn't consider myself as a literacy leader, I was able to lead our grade-level effort to support our students in acquiring disciplinary literacy across the curriculum.

Being a leader isn't always about doing it yourself, it's about setting the vision and then bringing in the right people to accomplish the goals. Leadership is about bringing out the expertise and strengths of the teachers in your team, not about what your expertise is. As the famous saying goes, "It's not about role; it's always about the goal."

Used with permission from Sharon Wright

the team has an equal voice and the power to contribute to decision-making. This allows barriers to dissolve and a team approach to prevail within the school. It is when teacher leaders are empowered to learn and lead with their colleagues that the most professional growth occurs. Teacher leaders must be willing to be learners themselves and have the skills and competencies to share their learning with others. Former ASCD executive director Judy Seltz observed:

> What happens in schools is more complex than ever and cannot be accomplished with strict division between administrators and teachers. The leadership and responsibility for student learning must be a collaborative effort. If teacher leaders can help change school cultures so that teachers and principals collaborate to build a culture of learning, everyone benefits. (ASCD, 2015, p. 5)

Figure 6.4. Reflection of an ELA Teacher Leader

Diana Liu, English Teacher
Brooklyn Technical High School
New York, NY

My philosophy of leadership is one in which everyone's strengths are valued. Building relationships with colleagues is essential to leadership and establishing a school culture of support, empowerment, and growth. When people feel appreciated and valued, they are also more likely to hold themselves to higher standards. This requires work at every level of the school and the willingness to adapt to change as the world in which schools exist is also continuously evolving.

For example, my own leadership was strengthened through my initial participation in classroom visits through the Learning Partners' Program. Subsequently, I led the development of a similar protocol for our school with my colleagues. This experience allowed me to learn among colleagues and welcome teachers to my classroom, leading by example for English disciplinary practices. Our teachers now have context to provide professional feedback to become better pedagogues, grow professionally, and increase collaboration in a large English department.

In the summer of 2017, I took on a last-minute instructional position as an ELL instructor at Brooklyn College for a group of Beijing students. The following academic year, I shared with my colleagues possibilities for forging collaborative international student-partnerships. Had I not stepped outside of my comfort zone that summer, I would not have necessarily thought about how we can incorporate multicultural inquiry instruction transnationally. Therefore, I would advise teachers who want to be leaders to begin examining issues present at your school, with a student-centered lens, and always rise to leadership opportunities that are presented. One way to begin doing this is to offer to lead professional development sessions with your disciplinary team.

Used with permission from Diana Liu

Reflect: Compare and contrast the three teacher leader reflections. How do you relate to their stories?

SUMMARY

This final chapter focused on how you can support your students to Share, Publish, and Act as they finalize their PBI process. Paolo Freire, a famous literacy scholar from Brazil, called action based on information *praxis* (Freire & Macedo, 1987). Equipping and empowering students to take action on socially significant issues in the disciplines shifts the paradigm from students learning from literacy critics, scientists, historians, and mathematicians to students becoming literacy critics, scientists, historians, and mathematicians.

Additionally, we encourage you to develop your path to become a change agent within the educational system. Being a teacher leader is both professionally challenging and satisfying, with benefits that are immeasurable for you and your students.

NOW IT'S YOUR TURN!

Plan your showcase for your students to share their PBI products. See Chapter 4 for ideas for your showcase. Also, plan how you will become a teacher leader for disciplinary literacy within your class, your school, and beyond.

Appendices

Appendix A: PBI Disciplinary Literacy Lesson for ELA

Appendix B: PBI Disciplinary Literacy Lesson for Science

Appendix C: PBI Disciplinary Literacy Lesson for History

Appendix D: PBI Disciplinary Literacy Lesson for Mathematics

Appendix E: PBI Disciplinary Literacy Lesson Template

The appendices contain sample lesson plans for inquiry-based disciplinary literacy for ELA, science, history/social studies, and mathematics, as well as a template that can be used with any disciplinary or interdisciplinary topic. The lessons are also available online in an expanded version for your convenience:

- *English/Language Arts*—tinyurl.com/PBIDLELA
- *Science*—tinyurl.com/PBIDLScience
- *History/Social Studies*—tinyurl.com/PBIDLhistory
- *Mathematics*—tinyurl.com/PBIDLmath
- *Template*—tinyurl.com/DLPBItemplate

PBI Disciplinary Literacy Lesson for ELA

See tinyurl.com/PBIDLELA

THE POWER OF LANGUAGE

Introduction/Overview

This is an inquiry lesson embedded in an overarching unit reading *I Am Malala* with a group of 9th- to 10th-grade students. The lesson integrates skills from the Common Core State Standards and components of the PBI cycle specific to disciplinary literacy in ELA. It provides key documents, websites, and instructional strategies that will provide teachers with an example of how disciplinary literacy functions in an ELA classroom. For this lesson, students are asked to explore how words impact people. They will analyze three different genres: vignette, poetry, and speech, which they will then creatively synthesize into their own speech directed toward their peer.

Texts

I Am Malala (available in audiobook and junior versions)
Malala Yousafzai's United Nations Speech, 2013
Selected chapters from *The House on Mango Street* by Sandra Cisneros
Selected Poems: "Manifesto" by Ellen Hopkins, "Perhaps" by Shu Ting, and student choice

ALIGNMENT TO COMMON CORE STATE STANDARDS

Students need opportunities to work with a variety of text types that represent high-quality examples of specific genres within the disciplines. *What types of text will you use in this lesson?*

Literature	Informational Text	Periodical Article	Informational Website	Blog	Personal Narrative	Poetry	Nonlinguistic Representation	Speech	Other
✓	✓				✓	✓		✓	

Common Core State Standards for ELA and Literacy in History/Social Studies, Science, and Technical Subjects

	9–10.1	9–10.2	9–10.3	9–10.4	9–10.5	9–10.6	9–10.7	9–10.8	9–10.9	9–10.10
Reading: Literature				✓						
Reading: Informational Text				✓						
Writing				✓						
Speaking & Listening			✓	✓						
Language					✓					

The PBI Model

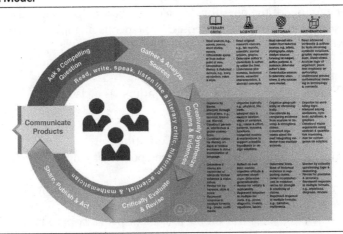

See Figure 2.1 on pp. 24–25 for a larger version

ASK A COMPELLING QUESTION

Lesson #1: The Inquiry Process

Domain-Specific Vocabulary:

Impact/Effect, Nonlinguistic

Learning Outcomes

Students will be able to:

- Understand how genre impacts the way a text is read.
- Analyze how diction (word choice) impacts the tone and, therefore, meaning.
- Analyze how shifts in genre, diction, or attitude affect meaning.
- Synthesize across multiple sources to create new ideas about the power of language.
- Choose words and rhetorical devices when writing to create an impact.

For this lesson, the inquiry question is teacher-developed, and the hook is used at the beginning of the lesson to help students examine why the inquiry question is important:

- Malala says the pen is mightier than the sword. Others say sticks and stones may break my bones but words will never hurt me. What do you think? Can words impact people?

Directions

Hook:

- Teacher will project the compelling question. In order to show understanding of the question, students will create a nonlinguistic representation of one of the quotes: "The pen is mightier than the sword."
  - ✓ Give students 5 minutes to draw their response/reaction/ interpretation of the quote.
  - ✓ Discuss and share visual representations as a class.

Activity:

- Explain the inquiry method and the question.
  - ✓ Students will be thinking about the power of language throughout the inquiry process.
  - ✓ Show students the PBI Model. Explain that in different disciplines, we conduct investigations a little bit differently.
- Students will create a free online journal at penzu.com to keep a research journal and record ideas during the inquiry process.

Closing:

- Students can ask any questions they have about the inquiry process.

When you read, write, speak, and listen like a literary critic:

Ask a Compelling Question	
Gather & Analyze Sources	• Read primary sources, such as novels, poems, short stories, essays. • Differentiate speaker from author point of view; analyze author's voice and style. • Understand the literal-level meaning of text. • Identify and interpret literary and rhetorical devices—for example, irony, symbolism, archetypal themes.
Creatively Synthesize Claims & Evidence	• Organize by genre or theme. • Interpret through critical lens—for instance, feminist, historical, Marxist. • Construct personal, intertextual, and global connections. • Construct claims for literary critique with textual evidence and close examination of language.
Critically Evaluate & Revise	• Monitor by revisiting question and aligning evidence to claims. • Determine if claims are supported with adequate textual evidence and elaboration. • Revise for coherence and style. • Represent response in multiple formats, such as prose and multimedia.
Share, Publish, & Act	

GATHER AND ANALYZE SOURCES

Lesson #2: Close Analytical Reading

Domain-Specific Vocabulary:

Genre, Expository, Diction

Hook:

- How does genre affect the way we read?
  - ✓ Students will record their initial thoughts in their online journal.
  - ✓ Review how we read differently in different disciplines.
  - ✓ Explain that we also read differently within English class depending on the genre.
- Students will read an excerpt from Chapters 8 and 15 of M. J. Adler's classic *How to Read a Book*.

✓ Students will underline main ideas and write an *E* in the margins for *expository texts* and a *P* in the margins for *poetry*.
✓ Add notes to their online journal.

Activity: Close Analytic Reading of Poetry

Model:

- Model a close reading of "Manifesto" by Ellen Hopkins for the class.
  ✓ Display the poem on the screen and have one student read the poem aloud for the class.
  ✓ Ask students for initial reactions to the poem.
  ✓ Guide students through a close analysis reading of the poem using TPS-CASST. (Directions below).

Guided Practice:

- Have students analyze "Perhaps" by Shu Ting in small groups. Conduct a close reading of the poem following the protocol for TPS-CASST as in the model.
- As a class, discuss how the author's choice of structure (second stanza repeats structure of first stanza but is more optimistic, third stanza contains theme, hanging indention emphasizes the word *perhaps*) and words (*perhaps* means uncertainty but it also means hope, *irresistible* has positive connotation) impacts meaning.

Independent Practice:

- Have students search and find their own poem concerning: knowledge, power, language, courage, oppression, education, and so forth, and complete their own close reading and analysis of the poem using TPS-CASST. (Example poems include "The Joy of Writing" by Szymborska and "The Rose that Grew from Concrete" by Tupac).

Closing

- Discuss how students can use diction (intentionally choosing certain words) to add meaning in their own writing.

TPS-CASTT Method of Poetry Analysis

Title: Examine the title before reading the poem. Sometimes the title will give you a clue about the content of the poem. In some cases, the title will give you crucial information that will help you understand a major idea within the poem.

Paraphrase: Paraphrase the literal action within the poem. At this point, resist the urge to jump into interpretation. A failure to understand what happens literally inevitably leads to an interpretive misunderstanding.

Speaker: Who is the speaker in the poem? Remember to always distinguish the speaker from the poet. In some cases, the speaker and the poet might be the same, but often, the speaker and the poet are entirely different.

Connotation: Examine the poem for figurative language, language that is not used literally. This would include, but is certainly not limited to, literary devices (symbolism, metaphors, litotes, allusion, irony) and the effect of sound devices (alliteration, onomatopoeia, assonance, consonance, rhyme, repetition).

Attitude (Tone): Tone refers to the speaker's attitude toward the subject of the poem. Of course, this means that you must discern the subject of the poem. In some cases, it may be narrow, and in others it will be broad. Also keep in mind the speaker's attitude toward self, other characters, and the subject. Look at the author's word choice (diction) to determine tone.

Shifts: Note shifts in speaker and attitude. Shifts can be indicated in a number of ways, including the occasion of the poem (time and place); key turn words (*but, yet*); punctuation (dashes, periods, colons); stanza divisions; changes in line of stanza length; and anything else that indicates that something has changed or a question is being answered.

Title: Examine the title again, this time on an interpretive level.

Theme: First, list what the poem is about (subject), and then determine what the poet is saying about each of those subjects (themes). Remember that the theme must be expressed as a complete sentence. The theme is the author's message about life.

GATHER AND ANALYZE SOURCES

Lesson #3: Locating Textual Evidence

Domain-Specific Vocabulary:

Vignette, Character, Tone, Theme

Directions

Hook:

- Review genre (exposition, poetry, memoir, personal narrative) by creating a List, Group, and Label or create a mindmap using the web application Text2MindMap.

Activity: Close Reading One Chapter from *The House on Mango Street*

- Introduce definition of vignette to students:
  - ✓ A vignette is a short, well-written sketch or descriptive scene.

✓ It doesn't have a plot, which would make it a story unto itself, but it does reveal something about the elements in it. It may reveal details about the character, tone, or theme.

Model:

- In an interview, Sandra Cisneros stated that many of the chapters in *The House on Mango Street* started as poems. She converted them to prose for the novella, but they still have many of the elements of poetry. As a class, talk about the similarities and differences between reading a lyric poem and reading a story (diction leads to tone in both, read for theme in both, deeper characterization in stories).
- Teacher reads "My Name."
    - ✓ Pause to think aloud about textual evidence revealing character, tone, and theme during the reading.
    - ✓ Show the students how to mark the text for evidence (both Ezperanzas are strong like a horse, fragmented storytelling leads to a childlike tone reflecting narrator's age and fragmented knowledge of her own identity and the world).

Guided Practice:

- Divide students into two groups where they will read one chapter ("A Smart Cookie" or "Alice Who Sees Mice") and draw connections to *I Am Malala*.
    - ✓ First, have students close-read their chapter individually, looking for details about the character, tone, or theme, and marking the textual evidence.
    - ✓ Then, in groups, have students identify ways in which Cisneros portrays women's identity, place in society, and importance of education in their chapter.
        - » Do women in this story have an identity? If so, what is it? If not, why not, and who seems to be "taking it away" from them? In contrast, how are the men portrayed in the vignette?
        - » What is/are the theme/s of the vignette?
    - ✓ On Padlet, students will record responses about themes (identity, role of women, and education).

Independent Practice:

- Ask students to add connections to themes in *I Am Malala* on the Padlet.

Closing

- Four Corners:
    - ✓ While students are adding intertextual connections to the Padlet, place a sign in each corner of the room: (1) strongly agree, (2) agree, (3) disagree, (4) strongly disagree.

✓ Direct students to go the corner of the room that matches their belief about the following statement: Women and men are equal.
✓ Students discuss why they chose that corner with other peers in the same corner; then they should choose a spokesperson for their group.
✓ The spokespeople take turns sharing the beliefs of their corners.
✓ After the spokespeople talk, direct students to move to a different corner if their belief has changed. The corner with the most "converts" wins.

GATHER AND ANALYZE SOURCES

Lesson #4: Analyzing Malala's Speech

Domain-Specific Vocabulary:

Rhetorical Devices, Parallel Structure, Allusion

Directions

This lesson is intended to take place after students have read Part 1 of *I Am Malala*.

Hook:

* Choose a quote and prove that it is true or prove that it isn't true in your online journal. You can use your own personal experiences or related readings to form your argument.

> "Only the educated are free."
>
> —Epictetus
>
> "The beautiful thing about learning is that no one can take it away from you."
>
> —B. B. King
>
> "I believe that education is the fundamental method of social progress and reform."
>
> —John Dewey
>
> "Establishing lasting peace is the work of education; all politics can do is keep us out of war."
>
> —Maria Montessori

* Discuss ideas as a class.

Activity: Speech Analysis

Model:

* Have students watch the UN Speech by Malala (17 minutes): youtube.com/watch?v=3rNhZu3ttIU
* While they are watching, model taking notes on:
  ✓ Her main argument;

    ✓ How she portrays her point; and

    ✓ What she says about women, education, and power.

- After watching the speech, discuss the speech as a class. Delineate Malala's main argument on the board or Google Docs.
    - ✓ Summarize the main claims of the speech.
    - ✓ How does she develop her argument?
    - ✓ What surprised the students?
    - ✓ What impressed them?

Guided Practice:

- Hand out a copy of Malala's speech for students to read: secure. aworldatschool.org/page/content/the-text-of-malala-yousafzais-speech-at-the-united-nations
- In small groups, have them analyze the speech for:
    - ✓ Rhetorical devices (i.e., parallel structure, repetition, allusion, word choice);
    - ✓ Specific evidence she uses to support her argument; and
    - ✓ What ideas from the beginning of her speech are included or expanded in her conclusion.
- Come back together as a class and discuss the rhetorical devices and how they create tone and meaning in the speech as a whole. Does the speech make an impact?

Closing

- Go back to the hook and have students discuss how their quote relates to Malala's speech.

CREATIVELY SYNTHESIZE CLAIMS AND EVIDENCE

Lesson #5: Say What You Need to Say

Directions

Hook:

Listen to the song "Say" by John Mayer.

Activity Prompt

Using the inquiry question (How can words impact people?) to guide your thinking, write a speech to your peers about the impact of words using your personal experience, observations, class readings, and/or knowledge of history.

    Your speech can answer any of the following questions:

- What is power and what power, if any, does language have?
- Can writers change the world?
- How do authors use language to stimulate complex thoughts and emotions?
- What makes a good speech?

As you write your speech, remember to do the following:

- Choose words to convey the appropriate tone.
- Consider the purpose, context, and audience for your speech.
- Be sure to clearly state your claims.
- Maintain your focus.
- Address any opposing claims.
- Edit your speech for tone and usage.

Brainstorming:

Have students create a triple Venn diagram based on the quotes, knowledge, and discussion from the different pieces of literature. They must combine at least three pieces of literature from this unit: *I Am Malala,* Malala's speech, *The House on Mango Street,* "Perhaps," or their selected poem.

Ways to synthesize ideas:

- Genre
- Theme
- Other literary devices

CRITICALLY EVALUATE AND REVISE

Lesson #6: Quality Control

Directions:

- Students self-evaluate using rubric.
- Experts in the field evaluate using rubric and give feedback to students.
- Students make revisions.

Rubric for Speech: The Impact of Words

Category	1: Above Standards	2: Meeting Standards	3: Approaching Standards	4: Below Standards	Score
Audience	Demonstrates a clear understanding of the potential reader and uses appropriate vocabulary and arguments. Anticipates reader's questions and provides thorough answers appropriate for that audience.	Demonstrates a general understanding of the potential reader and uses vocabulary and arguments appropriate for that audience.	Demonstrates some understanding of the potential reader and uses arguments appropriate for that audience.	It is not clear whom the author is writing for.	
Statement of Claim	The position statement provides a clear, strong statement of the author's position on the topic.	The position statement provides a clear statement of the author's position on the topic.	A position statement is present, but does not make the author's position clear.	There is no position statement.	
Evidence of Examples	All of the evidence and examples are specific and relevant, and explanations are given that show how each piece of evidence supports the author's position.	Most of the evidence and examples are specific and relevant, and explanations are given that show how each piece of evidence supports the author's position.	At least one of the pieces of evidence and examples is relevant and has an explanation that shows how that piece of evidence supports the author's position.	Evidence and examples are NOT relevant AND/OR are not explained.	
Word Choice	All words are well chosen to convey a clear and consistent tone.	Most words convey a clear tone.	Most words are appropriate, but there is an inconsistent or unclear tone.	Some words are not appropriate for the audience and/or tone.	

Rubric for Speech: The Impact of Words (continued)

Category	1: Above Standards	2: Meeting Standards	3: Approaching Standards	4: Below Standards	Score
Sources	All sources used for quotes, ideas, and facts are credible and cited correctly. The author cites at least three readings from class.	All sources used for quotes, ideas, and facts are credible and most are cited correctly. The author cites at least two readings from class.	All sources used for quotes, ideas, and facts are credible and are cited. The author cites at least two readings.	Some sources are suspect (not credible) and/or not cited. The author cites fewer than two readings.	

SHARE, PUBLISH, AND ACT

Lesson #7: Social Media for Social Justice

Directions

After students have revised and polished their speeches, they will create a VoiceThread recording of their speech, adding images that mirror the tone. Students will share their work with their classmates, parents, and community.

The teacher will encourage students to continuously engage through social media.

Twitter Conversations

- #ThePenIsMightierThanTheSword
- #IAmMalala
- #theworldneedsmoreeducation

Facebook

- I Am Malala community: facebook.com/iammalalabook
- UN Girls Ed Initiative: facebook.com/UNGEI

A World at School

- Stand with Malala petition: aworldatschool.org/iammalala
- @aworldatschool: Show us your best #IAmMalala photo of you raising your hand with "I am Malala" on it. Post it on Instagram, Facebook, or Twitter and include #iamMalala.
- Youth Advocacy Kits: issuu.com/globaleducationfirst/docs/youth_advocacy_toolkit_full_large

—by Abbey Graham and Shea Kerkhoff

PBI Disciplinary Literacy Lesson for Science

See tinyurl.com/PBIDLScience

OUR RIVER BASINS

Introduction/Overview

This is an inquiry lesson embedded in an overarching unit reading *A Civil Action* in Earth and Environmental Science with a group of 9th-grade students. The lesson integrates skills from the Essential State Standards and components of the inquiry cycle specific to disciplinary literacy in science. It provides key terminology, websites, and instructional strategies that will provide teachers with an example of how disciplinary literacy functions in a science classroom. For this lesson, students are asked to explore a river basin in their state. They will then creatively synthesize into their own informational and evaluative presentation directed toward their peers.

Texts

A Civil Action nonfiction narrative on water contamination
"Freshwater Crisis" online article
River basin map
USGS Water Quality Data

ALIGNMENT TO STANDARDS

Thinking About Text Types

Students need opportunities to work with a variety of text types that represent high-quality examples of specific genres within the disciplines. *What types of text will you use in this lesson?*

Literature	Informational Text	Periodical Article	Informational Website	Blog	Narrative	Poetry	Nonlinguistic Representation	Speech	Other
			✓		✓		✓		

Common Core State Standards for Literacy in Science and Technical Subjects

	9–10.1	9–10.2	9–10.3	9–10.4	9–10.5	9–10.6	9–10.7	9–10.8	9–10.9	9–10.10
Reading: Science and Technical Text	✓								✓	
Writing		✓		✓	✓	✓	✓			

The PBI Model

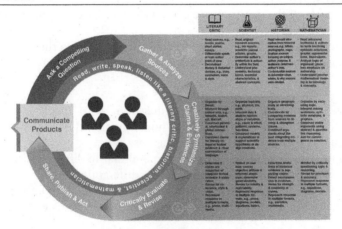

See Figure 2.1 on pp. 24–25 for a larger version

ASK A COMPELLING QUESTION

Lesson #1: The Inquiry Process

Domain-Specific Vocabulary:

Hydrosphere, Water Quality

Learning Outcomes

Students will be able to do the following:

- Analyze the parts of a river.
- Explore a river basin's structure and processes.
- Synthesize across multiple sources to create new ideas about river basins.
- Evaluate how humans use water.
- Evaluate human influences on water quality in our state's river basins.
- Support claims with textual evidence to create a compelling presentation.

For this lesson, the compelling question is teacher-developed. Students will choose which river basin to study.

- How do humans influence water pollution in our state's river basins?

Directions

Hook:

- Teacher will project the Compelling Question. In order to show importance of the question, the class will review the Moburn, Massachusetts, case.
    - ✓ Give students 2 minutes to predict water quality in their state.
    - ✓ Discuss and share predictions as a class.

Activity:

- Explain the inquiry method and the question.
    - ✓ Students will be thinking about how humans influence water quality throughout the inquiry process.
    - ✓ Show students the PBI Model. Explain that in different disciplines, we conduct investigations a little bit differently.
- Students will create a free online journal at penzu.com to keep a research journal and record ideas during the inquiry process.

Closing:

- Students can ask any questions they have about the inquiry process.

When you read, write, speak, and listen like a scientist:

Ask a Compelling Question	
Gather & Analyze Sources	• Read original research sources, such as lab reports and scientific journal articles.
	• Determine author's credentials and authority within a field; analyze rigor of methods.

Gather & Analyze Sources (continued)	• Understand technical terms, essential characteristics, and abstract concepts. • Look for negative space in order to generate hypothesis.
Creatively Synthesize Claims & Evidence	• Organize by topic, such as physical, life, earth. • Interpret data and analyze relationships of variables. • Aim for consensus in scientific community. • Construct models and explanations to support scientific hypothesis or design solutions.
Critically Evaluate & Revise	• Monitor by reflecting on own bias; convey objective attitude and informed skepticism; determine generalizability. • Determine if claims are supported with adequate textual evidence. • Revise for validity and replicability. • Represent response in multiple formats—for example, prose, diagrams, models, equations, tables.

Share, Publish, & Act

GATHER & ANALYZE SOURCES

Lesson #2: Locating Textual Evidence

Domain-Specific Vocabulary:

River Basin, Headwaters, Tributaries, Watershed, Discharge, Precipitation

Hook:

Watch the video on the home page of water-alliance.org. Explain that the video gives important points but not specific facts backed up by textual evidence.

Activity

Explicit Instruction

Teacher gives Prezi on parts of a river and the water cycle process. For each set of facts, the teacher goes to the original webpage and shows students where the information came from and shows how the teacher knew the sources were reliable. Teacher gives explicit instruction on locating textual evidence from reliable sources.

Reliable Sources

• Credentials of author
• Funding source disclosed and not a conflict of interest
• Most recent data

- Convergence with scientific consensus
- Valid and reliable evidence

Types of Textual Evidence

- Experiment results
- Observations that used scientific method
- Statistics
- Scientific consensus as a fact

Guided Practice:

In small groups, the students read the article "Freshwater Crisis—Why It Matters" shown below. The students determine if the source is credible by following the link and supporting their decision with evidence from the webpage. The students then read the article and highlight the textual evidence: pink for experiment results, yellow for observations, orange for statistics, blue for scientific consensus as fact.

Independent Practice:

Students will explore a river basin of their choice using a river basin interactive map. The students will also explore the links given by the website at the bottom of each River Basin webpage. Students will analyze data on the USGS Interactive Real-Time Data Map linked below and explore the USGS website: water.usgs.gov/edu/waterquality.html. Students must analyze one additional reliable source for the presentation.

Example of the North Carolina Environmental River Basin Map:
   eenorthcarolina.org/riverbasins-interactive.html
USGS Interactive Real-Time Data Map: nc.water.usgs.gov/realtime

Freshwater Crisis—Why It Matters

Posted by the Clean Water Americas Alliance:

Although nearly 70 percent of the globe is covered by water, environmentalists and specialists all over the world constantly talk about water crisis. That is because only 2.5 percent of all the water on earth is fresh water, the rest of it being ocean based and saline. Furthermore, out of those 2.5 percent, only 1 percent can be easily accessed, the rest being trapped in snowfields and glaciers. If you make a simple mathematic calculus, you will see that, basically, only 0.007 percent of the water on our planet is available for 6.8 billion people. That is what constitutes a crisis. The water we drink has been present on this earth for hundreds of millions of years, in one form or another, being continuously recycled through the atmosphere. Therefore, the amount of freshwater has remained somewhat constant, while the population of the planet exploded. To that extent, as years go by, the competition for clean water, better yet a sufficient supply of clean water for drinking, maintaining a proper hygiene or even sustaining life growth becomes more and more intense.

Because water scarcity is an abstract concept to a large part of the world's population, few people realize why the freshwater crisis matters, except of course for those who live in that stark reality. However, the extent of its importance is quite simple: water is life. Geography and climate, but also the competition for resources, engineering and regulations have made it so that some parts of the planet enjoy great supplies of freshwater, while others have debilitating pollution and drought. But people need water to survive, not just in the sense of drinking water, but also clean water for cooking, hygiene needs and also keeping the environment clean.

In Africa, 4,000 children die every year from diarrhea, because they have no hygienic toilets and clean water to wash their hands. A simple condition like diarrhea, which could be easily fixed if there were a supply of clean water, kills more children than diseases like AIDS and malaria. Humans have proven to be inefficient water users, spending about 2,400 liters of clean water to produce a hamburger and growing water intensive crops, like cotton, in arid regions.

The freshwater crisis matters not only from today's perspective and the fact that people in developing countries are practically dying from clean water scarcity, but also because the future looks grim. Estimations show that by the year 2025, water scarcity will affect about 1.8 billion people and two thirds of the world will be living in water stressed regions. So humans now face another challenge, to effectively conserve and manage water resources, as well as distributing the supplies of fresh water we have, especially since solutions are greatly affected by climate, policy, technology and people alike. Nevertheless, it is important to remember that the freshwater crisis is a global issue and it matters or it should matter for everybody, even though some parts of the world enjoy a flush of clean water supplies at the moment.

Retrieved from cleanwateramericaalliance.org/
category/clean-water-crisis

CREATIVELY SYNTHESIZE CLAIMS & EVIDENCE

Lesson #3: Facts and Opinions

Activity Prompt

Using the compelling question to guide your thinking, give a Prezi presentation to your peers about a river basin in our state.

Your presentation should address all of the following questions:

- What is the name of the river basin you chose?
- What counties does it affect?

- How long is the basin?
- How do humans use water in this basin?
- What is the water quality of this basin?
- How do humans influence the water quality of this river basin?

As you write, remember to do the following:

- Consider the purpose and audience for your presentation.
- Be sure to clearly state your claims.
- Support your claims with textual evidence.

Brainstorming:

Have students create a Fact | Opinion T-chart to make sure they have both the information and argumentation parts of the assignment. Then, have students draw a line to a fact that supports each of their opinions. If there is not a line, students need to do more research to support their opinions.

CRITICALLY EVALUATE & REVISE

Lesson #4: Quality Control

Directions:

- Students self-evaluate using rubric.
- Experts in the field evaluate using rubric and give feedback to students.
- Students make revisions.

Rubric for Presentation: How Do Humans Influence Water Pollution in North Carolina's River Basins?

Category	4: Above Standards	3: Meets Standards	2: Approaching Standards	1: Below Standards	Score
Informs Audience	Demonstrates a clear understanding of the audience. Informs the audience on the important facts of the topic. Defines terminology as needed.	Demonstrates a general understanding of the potential audience and uses important facts appropriate for that audience.	Demonstrates some understanding of the potential audience.	The terminology and facts are far below or far above the education level of the audience.	

Category	4: Above Standards	3: Meets Standards	2: Approaching Standards	1: Below Standards	Score
Statement of Claim	The position statement provides a clear, strong statement of the author's position on the topic.	The position statement provides a clear statement of the author's position on the topic.	A position statement is present, but does not make the author's position clear.	There is no position statement.	
Textual Evidence	All of the evidence and examples are specific and relevant. Explanations are given that show how each piece of evidence supports the author's position.	Most of the evidence and examples are specific and relevant, and explanations are given that show how each piece of evidence supports the author's position.	At least one of the pieces of evidence and examples is relevant and has an explanation that shows how that piece of evidence supports the author's position.	Evidence and examples are NOT relevant AND/OR are not explained.	
Sources	All sources used for evidence are credible and cited correctly. The author cites at least three readings from class.	All sources used for evidence are credible and most are cited correctly. The author cites at least two readings from class.	Most sources used for evidence are cited correctly. The author cites at least two readings from class.	Many sources are suspect (not credible) AND/OR are not cited correctly. The author cites fewer than two readings from class.	

SHARE, PUBLISH, & ACT

Lesson #5: Take a Stand

Directions

After students have revised and polished their presentations, they will share their Prezis with the community of that river basin by posting a link to the

Prezi on the students' own Facebook or Twitter pages or on one of the options below.

The teacher will encourage students to continuously engage in the conversation about water pollution in their state through social media. Examples for North Carolina are below:

Twitter

- @environmentNC
- @CleanWaterforNC

Facebook

- North Carolina Earth Share: facebook.com/EarthShareNC
- Help Preserve North Carolina Environment: facebook.com/environmentnorthcarolina
- Piedmont Environmental Alliance: facebook.com/peanc
- Southern Environmental Law Center: facebook.com/southernenvironment

—by Shea Kerkhoff

PBI Disciplinary Literacy Lesson for History

See tinyurl.com/PBIDLhistory

SUSPENDING DEATH:
LINCOLN, THE TELEGRAPH, AND MILITARY JUSTICE

Introduction/Overview

This lesson focuses on President Abraham Lincoln's approach to military justice. The lesson is designed to model the Inquiry Arc from the C3 Framework for State Standards in Social Studies. In the inquiry described in this lesson, students examine telegram messages Lincoln sent in 1864 and 1865 to better understand Lincoln's approach to military justice.

Texts

The Lincoln Telegrams: lincolntelegrams.com

Background

Reading the brief and deliberate telegram about John Abshier shown below, we can learn much about Abraham Lincoln—his temperament and his personality. Lincoln was a sensible and caring man, as well as stern, hands-on, equitable, and above revenge and the temptations of power. Telegrams that Lincoln sent in the last year of his presidency consistently suggest his strong loyalty to friends, family, and political supporters, and also his stubborn determination and careful attention to questions of justice in a time of war.

Executive Mansion, Washington, DC, March 17, 1864

Major General Rosecrans, St. Louis.

Suspend execution of death sentence of John F. Abshier, citizen, until further orders.

A. Lincoln, sent 12:10 P.M.

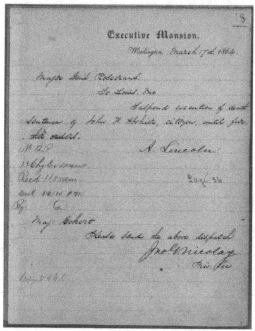

"Lincoln Telegram March 17, 1864" by Admin is licensed under CC BY-SA 3.0
Unported: wiki.lincolntelegrams.com/index.php?title=March_17,_1864

A significant number of Lincoln's telegrams concern the exercise of military justice, exchange of prisoners of war, and stays of execution. Researching the context of these telegrams reveals the gripping, complex politics and the morbid negotiations concerning prisoners of war in both Union and Confederate camps. Generals leveraged the lives of soldiers in power struggles, demanding the attention of Lincoln, who often responded to the pleas of distraught soldiers' wives and families. Several historical researchers, including Alotta (1990), Thompson (n.d.), Wittenberg (2012), and Homstad (2001), tell of Lincoln's involvement in negotiating the fates of soldiers and POWs.

Lincoln was regularly beset with letters and telegrams from families, politicians, army officers, and clergy, and his responses were most often urgent, calculated, and—sometimes—filled with despondency or frustration.

ALIGNMENT TO STANDARDS

Thinking About Text Types

Students need opportunities to work with a variety of text types that represent high-quality examples of specific genres within the disciplines. *What types of text will you use in this lesson?*

Literature	Informational Text	Periodical Article	Informational Website	Blog	Narrative	Poetry	Nonlinguistic Representation	Speech	Other
	✓	✓	✓		✓		✓		✓

Common Core State Standards for ELA and Literacy in History/Social Studies, Science, and Technical Subjects

	9–10.1	9–10.2	9–10.3	9–10.4	9–10.5	9–10.6	9–10.7	9–10.8	9–10.9	9–10.10
Reading in History/Social Studies:	✓	✓						✓	✓	
Reading in Science/Tech										
Writing	✓	✓	✓	✓	✓	✓	✓	✓		
Speaking & Listening										

The PBI Model

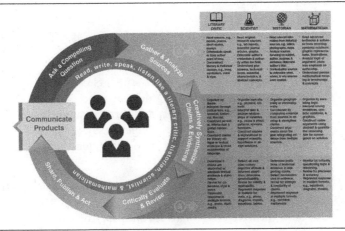

See Figure 2.1 on pp. 24–25 for a larger version

LESSON #1: ASK A COMPELLING QUESTION

Learning Outcomes

Students will be able to do the following:

- Closely read telegram memos written by President Abraham Lincoln in 1864 and 1865.
- Analyze the telegrams.
- Synthesize information gathered and analyzed related to President Lincoln's approach to military justice.

Inquiry Question

All inquiry begins with questions. The C3 Framework (socialstudies.org/ C3) recognizes that teachers and students both play an important role in the process of developing questions and then planning inquiry. Ultimately, students should be enabled to develop their own questions and situate those questions in the context of what we already know. Such work requires deep knowledge of facts, ideas, and the general context supporting the questions. Consequently, teachers should provide support and even models for students as they build their questioning skills.

For this lesson, students might be given the following compelling question as a starting place for planning the inquiry:

- How did Lincoln carry out wartime justice?

Students should read background material (see the Background Historical Sources, p. 124) to understand why this question is important and to get some ideas for how others have addressed the question. Students might even return to the question and revise or rewrite the question. As students read the background materials, they should write down other questions that occur to them. Students should ask what more they need to know about Lincoln, about the Civil War, and about prisoners of war to answer the compelling question. They should also think about what "hunches" they might have about how to answer the question.

With this background work completed, students should then shift to developing supporting questions that will guide the process of researching the compelling question and maybe even spark further questions. Supporting questions require explanations and are typically more factually oriented than compelling questions. Examples of supporting questions for this inquiry include these:

- What were some of the reasons why soldiers could be court-martialed during the Civil War?
- How many soldiers were court-martialed during the Civil War?
- How common were court-martials?

- For what reasons did Lincoln interfere with wartime justice?
- How many pardons did Lincoln issue?
- How many times did Lincoln request by telegram information about military justice cases?

With compelling and supporting questions in place, students should read some of the telegrams from Lincoln, including those that are listed below. In addition, students should read the analysis that accompanies these telegram messages. This analysis was conducted by students and teachers at North Carolina State University and is presented in a wiki format:

March 17, 1864: wiki.lincolntelegrams.com/index.php?title=March_17,
_1864

April 12, 1864: wiki.lincolntelegrams.com/index.php?title=April_12,_1864

December 27, 1864: wiki.lincolntelegrams.com/index.php?title=December
_27,_1864

February 1, 1865 (5): wiki.lincolntelegrams.com/index.php?title=February
_1,_1865_(5)

February 9, 1865 (2): wiki.lincolntelegrams.com/index.php?title=February
_9,_1865_(2)

March 20, 1865 (3): wiki.lincolntelegrams.com/index.php?title=March
_20,_1865_(3)

April 11, 1865: wiki.lincolntelegrams.com/index.php?title=April_11,_1865

As students read the telegrams and the related analysis, they should take notes using a graphic organizer such as the one below. The organizer includes a place for students to begin the process of developing an answer to the compelling question. These initial responses will be more like a hunch or an impression that is emerging during the process.

	What am I learning from this telegram?	What more do I need to know?	What are my initial ideas or hunches?
Telegram 1			
Telegram 2			
Secondary Sources			

After reading and analyzing the telegram messages and analysis, students should use specific details or perspectives to determine the meaning and purposes of each telegram. As they conduct their analysis, students will apply disciplinary concepts and tools so they can write about the context in which the telegrams were written. This should include where and when the telegrams were produced and what was happening within the broader context of the Civil War.

LESSON #3: CREATIVELY SYNTHESIZE CLAIMS & EVIDENCE

As students read the telegrams, they will be evaluating historical information for the purpose of answering their compelling question. This process can be supported with additional questions such as: What is their gut feeling about Lincoln? Was he really a fair man, or do they think the telegrams suggest that he abused his power as president?

As the analysis continues, students should begin to develop some conclusions in response to the compelling question. In doing so, they should reflect on their research and findings:

- Did their conclusions match their hunches?
- What mysteries still lie in the telegrams?
- What other questions arose as a result of their research?

As students continue to refine their ideas, they should draft an initial response to the compelling question. This response should reflect the evidence students have located to support claims that emerged through research and corroboration. The writing process should continue with additional refinement and peer review.

Background Historical Sources

As a next step, students should assess their peers' responses to the compelling question, noting the common inferences, opinions, and results other students reached. As they critically review, students should consider questions such as these:

- What disagreements or variations did the students encounter?
- How does Lincoln's approach to military justice compare to that of other presidents?
- How does what they learned about Lincoln influence their thinking about military justice today? Consider high-profile cases such as those of Patrick Manning, the Guantanamo Detention Camp, and the Abu Ghraib torture case.

As a culminating activity, students should publish their analysis. The publishing process should consist of two activities. First, have students prepare a final draft of a report on their analysis as a response to the compelling question: *How did Lincoln carry out wartime justice?* The written response should include an appropriate amount of evidence drawn from the Background Historical Sources and from the telegrams. These final drafts should also reflect the critical evaluation and revision process. The follow criteria can be used to evaluate students' writing:

- A rich description of the content of Lincoln's use of the telegraph:
  - ✓ Extent of Lincoln's use of telegrams
  - ✓ Types of activities and events Lincoln managed using the telegraph

- Minimum of three high-level claims about Lincoln's use of the telegrams and his approach to military justice
- Inclusion of evidence to support claims taken from both historical background sources and from telegrams
- Clearly written with limited grammatical errors

A second activity would be for students to adapt their written work into an alternative format using an emerging technology. This adaptation should reflect Lincoln's creative and forward-thinking use of what was at the time an emerging technology in the telegraph. Some platforms for publishing include the following:

- Twitter (see our Lincoln Telegram Twitter page as an example (twitter. com/lincolntelegram)
- Pinterest
- Facebook

—by Miranda Danku

PBI Disciplinary Literacy Lesson for Mathematics

See tinyurl.com/PBIDLmath

AVERAGE MONTHLY TEMPERATURE

Introduction/Overview

This is an inquiry lesson for mathematics that addresses standards that are now required for all students: trigonometric functions and modeling. The lesson integrates skills from the Common Core State Standards for Mathematics and components of the inquiry cycle specific to disciplinary literacy in mathematics. It provides key terminology, websites, and instructional strategies that will provide teachers with an example of how disciplinary literacy functions in a mathematics classroom. For this lesson, students are asked to explore average monthly temperature data for a U.S. city of their choosing. They will then harness the power of technology to investigate how to model these data using a trigonometric equation and keep a journal detailing their findings. Through this investigation, they will explore how different parameters influence the graph of cosine and sine. They will also analyze a mathematics text to revise their conjectures, evaluate the writing of their peers, and create a final product based on their experience during the lesson.

Texts

Temperature Data: weatherbase.com/weather/state.php3?c=US
Mathematics Text: classzone.com/eservices/home/pdf/student/LA214EAD. pdf

Mathematics Technology

Core-Math Tools: nctm.org/coremathtools

ALIGNMENT TO STANDARDS

Thinking About Text Types

Students need opportunities to work with a variety of text types that represent high-quality examples of specific genres within the disciplines. *What types of text will you use in this lesson?*

Literature	Informational Text	Periodical Article	Informational Website	Blog	Narrative	Poetry	Nonlinguistic Representation	Speech	Other
	✓		✓	✓			✓		✓

Common Core State Standards for ELA and Literacy in History/Social Studies, Science, and Technical Subjects

	9–10.1	9–10.2	9–10.3	9–10.4	9–10.5	9–10.6	9–10.7	9–10.8	9–10.9	9–10.10
Reading: Science/Text			✓	✓	✓		✓		✓	
Writing	✓	✓		✓	✓	✓	✓		✓	
Speaking & Listening	✓			✓	✓					

This lesson is also aligned with the Common Core State Standards for Mathematics:

The Modeling Standards and High School →
Functions → Trigonometric Functions → B.5

The PBI Model

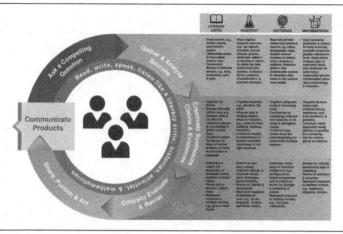

See Figure 2.1 on pp. 24–25 for a larger version

ASK A COMPELLING QUESTION

Lesson #1: The Inquiry Process

Domain-Specific Vocabulary:

Average Daily Temperature, Cyclic, Periodic, Trigonometric Function

Learning Outcomes

Students will be able to do the following:

- Model weather data using trigonometric functions.
- Explore average monthly temperature for a U.S. city.
- Synthesize across multiple data points to understand how certain parameters of an equation influences its graph.
- Evaluate the parameters for trigonometric functions.
- Use textual evidence to support claims following an investigation.
- Support claims with evidence from an investigation to create a compelling presentation.
- Analyze data to model real-world climate statistics and make conclusions based on comparisons.

Ask a Compelling Question

For this lesson, the inquiry question is teacher-developed. Students will choose which U.S. city they want to study.

- How can the average monthly temperature for a U.S. city be modeled using mathematics?

Directions

Hook:

- Teacher will project the compelling question: How can the average monthly temperature for a U.S. city be modeled using mathematics?
  - ✓ Ask students what is meant by *average monthly temperature*.
  - ✓ Give students 1 minute to predict what a graph of the average monthly temperatures for a city might look like.
  - ✓ Discuss and share predictions as a class.
  - ✓ Show the class the webpage usclimatedata.com/climate/new-york/new-york/united-states/usny0996 and discuss the weather data for New York City.
  - ✓ Describe what it means for data to be cyclic or periodic.

Activity:

- Explain the inquiry method and the question.
  - ✓ Through the inquiry process, students will be discovering how to use trigonometric functions (cosine and sine) to model temperature data.
  - ✓ Show students the PBI Model. Explain that in different disciplines, we conduct investigations a little bit differently and in this mathematics investigation we will be modeling trig functions.
  - ✓ Show students the model shown below. Explain the links between the inquiry process and what it takes to read, write, and speak like a mathematician.
- Students will create a free online journal at penzu.com to keep an investigation journal and record ideas during the inquiry process.

Closing:

- Students can ask any questions they have about the inquiry process.

When you read, write, speak, and listen like a mathematician:

Ask a Compelling Question	
Gather & Analyze Sources	• Read advanced textbooks and real-life texts involving symbolic notations, graphic representations, illustrations, and so on. • Analyze the logic of argument with less attention to authorship. • Understand the precise mathematical meaning in terminology and concepts.
Creatively Synthesize Claims & Evidence	• Organize tangentially. • Navigate among and interpret sentences, symbolic notations, and graphic representations. • Look for and express regularity in repeated reasoning. • Construct viable arguments using abstract and quantitative reasoning.
Critically Evaluate & Revise	• Monitor by critically questioning logic and reasoning. • Revise for precision. • Represent response in multiple formats, such as equations, diagrams, models, tables, and so forth.
Share, Publish, & Act	

GATHER AND ANALYZE SOURCES

Lesson #2: Locating Data

Domain-Specific Vocabulary:

Parameter, Cosine Function, Sine Function

Hook:

Show the monthly average temperature for New York City: weather.com/weather/wxclimatology/monthly/graph/USNY0996. Make sure to show students the multiple representations of the data ("Table Display" and "Graph Display"). Explain that students are going to pick a city of their choosing and find temperature data for that city and then fit a trigonometric function to the data using technology tools.

Activity

Explicit Instruction:

Teacher shows students how to download and open the free Java-based Core-Math Tools program: nctm.org/coremathtools. Then the teacher instructs students to open the Computer Algebra System (CAS), the top application on the left under Algebra and Functions. As the teacher explains how to use the software application, important things to make sure the students understand are as follows:

- Once in the CAS, students need to open a new data window. To do this, click on "File" and then "Data," and then "New Data." This will enable both the CAS and spreadsheet features.
- In the "Y=" tab, have students enter the following:
  - ✓ $y=a*\cos(b*(x-h))+k$
  - ✓ It is important they enter it exactly as shown.
  - ✓ Explain that a, b, h, and k are parameters of the equation; they will be manipulated during the investigation.
  - ✓ Explain the difference between a variable (the x) and the parameters.
- The "Settings" tab can change the window of the graph.
- The "Graph" tab will plot a graph of the cosine function, and there will be sliders for each parameter. Give the students a couple of minutes to become familiar with the sliders, moving them back and forth and allowing them to see how it changes the graph. To change the range of a parameter, click on the letter of the parameter and enter the new range.
- The "Data" tab is where they will enter data for the city of their choosing. They should label column A "Month" and column B "Average Daily Temperature":
  - ✓ For "Month," we need quantitative data, so students should use 1, 2, 3, and so on to represent January, February, March, and so forth. If it is appropriate, you can discuss with students the difference between numerical (quantitative) and categorical (qualitative) data, but it is not imperative for the lesson. It is, however, important for students to know they have to use numbers to represent months so that they can graph the data and model them with a function.

Independent Practice:

Students will explore average monthly temperature data for a U.S. city of their choosing. Students will find the average monthly temperature online for the city of their choice. They can find their data from doing their own search online, or they may be directed to weatherbase.com/weather/state. php3?c=US. Once they pick their city and find appropriate data, they should enter it into the data tab of their Core-Math Tools. To plot their data, they should do the following:

- Click on the "Show Scatterplot" icon.
- The default column selections are appropriate for the data, so click "OK" when asked to choose columns.

Students should write in their Penzu journal about the city they found, the shape of the graph they are modeling, and any conjectures they have about the cosine function they will model.

CREATIVELY SYNTHESIZE CLAIMS AND EVIDENCE

Lesson #3: Investigation and Conjecturing

Activity Prompt

Using the inquiry question to guide your thinking, update your Penzu journal with what you discover about each parameter of the cosine function and the function that modeled the data for the city you chose.

To begin, students should go to the "Graph" tab and manipulate the parameters to model a cosine function to the data they gathered. Then, they should write in their journal according to the stipulations below.

Your journal should address all of the following questions:

- What is the name of the city you chose?
- What function models your temperature data?
- If you were to visit this city in the winter, what type of clothes would you need?
- If you were to visit this city in the summer, what type of clothes would you need?
- How did each of the parameters influence the graph of $y=\cos(x)$?
    - ✓ a
    - ✓ b
    - ✓ h
    - ✓ k
- How could you use your data to find each of the parameters? In other words, write an equation for finding each parameter.
- How would your function change if you wanted to model your data with a sine function? In the "Y=" tab, enter $y=a*\sin(b*(x-h))+k$.

As you write, remember to do the following:

- Be sure to state your conjectures clearly; it is okay if you revise them later.
- Support your claims with evidence from your investigation.
- Use precise mathematical terminology, including symbols and definitions.
- Use multiple representations as you explain your results: tables, graphs, equations, pictures, and so forth.

CRITICALLY EVALUATE AND REVISE

Lesson #4: Comparing to Texts and Peers

Students will self-evaluate findings from their investigation by reading a mathematics text and comparing their results to the textbook source. Then, they will revise their conjectures. Finally, students will compare their work with that of their peers to reach conclusions.

Directions

Students will read a mathematics text about trigonometric equations. One example can be found at classzone.com/eservices/home/pdf/student/LA214EAD.pdf. Alternatively, any standard precalculus book could be used. Here, students will learn the following terms: *sinusoidal, amplitude, period, horizontal shift*, and *vertical shift*. This technical reading will introduce them to the standard methods for finding the amplitude and period for trigonometric models. Students will learn to use appropriate symbols and terminology when working with trigonometric functions.

Next, students will revise their Penzu journal based on the findings of their reading. They will begin to finalize their argument for the compelling question as they revise their conjectures. If they need more exploration to attach meaning to what they read, they can open a new window in Core-Math Tools and explore how different parameters (when considered in isolation) influence the graph of $y=\cos(x)$. They should be encouraged to explore: $y=A*\cos(x)$, $y=\cos(B*x)$, $y=\cos(x\text{-}h)$, $y=\cos(x)+K$.

As a next step, students should assess their peers' responses to the compelling question, noting the common inferences and results other students reached. As they critically review, students should consider questions such as these:

- What similarities are there in students' reasoning?
- What disagreements or variations did the students encounter?
- How do their responses compare to the mathematical text?
- Why does their trigonometric function not exactly model the temperature data they collected?

SHARE, PUBLISH, AND ACT

Lesson #5: Reporting Findings

As a culminating activity, after students have revised their hypotheses based on the mathematics text and a review of their peers' work, students should publish their analysis. The publishing process should consist of two activities. First, students should prepare a final draft of a report on their analysis as a response to the compelling question: *How can the average monthly temperature for a U.S. city be modeled using mathematics?* The written response should include an appropriate amount of evidence drawn from the investigation and mathematics text. These final drafts should also reflect the critical evaluation and revision process. The following criteria can be used to evaluate students' writing:

- A rich description of how they used the technology features of Core-Math Tools to model the temperature data
- Their conclusions about how to find the amplitude and period for their equation
- Their interpretation about how to use the data to plan their outfits if they vacationed to the city during different seasons
- Inclusion of evidence to support their claims following the investigation and analysis of the mathematics text
- Clearly written with limited grammatical errors
- Proper use of mathematics symbols and definitions

The second activity is for students to adapt their written work into an alternative format using an emerging technology. This adaptation should reflect multiple representations of their data and how they can use trigonometric equations to model data. Some platforms for publishing include these:

- Twitter
- Pinterest
- Facebook
- Prezi

—by Erin Krupa

PBI Disciplinary Literacy Lesson Template

See tinyurl.com/DLPBItemplate

TITLE

Introduction/Overview

[provide a brief introduction to your IDL as well as an overview of the content of your IDL]

Texts

[list the texts you will use in your IDL]

ALIGNMENT TO COMMON CORE STATE STANDARDS

Step 3: Thinking About Text Types

Students need opportunities to work with a variety of text types that represent high-quality examples of specific genres within the disciplines. *What types of text will you use in this lesson?*

Literature	Informational Text	Periodical Article	Informational Website	Blog	Personal Narrative	Poetry	Nonlinguistic Representation	Speech	Other
✓									

Common Core State Standards for ELA and Literacy in History/Social Studies, Science, and Technical Subjects

	9–10.1	9–10.2	9–10.3	9–10.4	9–10.5	9–10.6	9–10.7	9–10.8	9–10.9	9–10.10
Reading	✓									
Writing										

The PBI Model

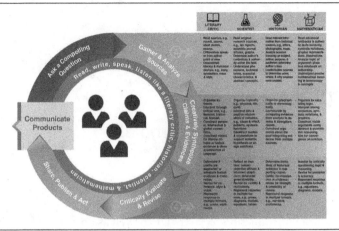

See Figure 2.1 on pp. 24–25 for a larger version

ASK A COMPELLING QUESTION:

Lesson #1: Introducing the IDL

Domain-Specific Vocabulary:

Learning Outcomes:

Students will be able to:

- (list the learning outcomes for your IDL here)

Ask a Compelling Question

Directions

Hook:

Activity:

Closing:

GATHER AND ANALYZE SOURCES

Lesson #2: Close Reading

Domain-Specific Vocabulary:

Hook:

Activity: Close Analytic Reading of Poetry

Model:

Guided Practice:

Independent Practice:

Closing

GATHER AND ANALYZE SOURCES
Lesson #3: Locating Textual Evidence

Domain-Specific Vocabulary:

Directions

Hook:

Activity: Close Reading of One Chapter from *The House on Mango Street*

Model:

Guided Practice:

Independent Practice:

Closing

CREATIVELY SYNTHESIZE CLAIMS AND EVIDENCE
Lesson #4

Directions

Hook:

Activity Prompt

Brainstorming:

CRITICALLY EVALUATE AND REVISE
Lesson #5

Directions

- Students self-evaluate using rubric.
- Experts in the field evaluate using rubric and give feedback to students.
- Students make revisions.

[Rubric for Sample: see next page]

SHARE, PUBLISH, AND ACT
Lesson #6

Rubric for Sample

Category	4: Above Standards	3: Meets Standards	2: Approaching Standards	1: Below Standards	Score
Audience	Demonstrates a clear understanding of the potential reader and uses appropriate vocabulary and arguments. Anticipates reader's questions and provides thorough answers appropriate for that audience.	Demonstrates a general understanding of the potential reader and uses vocabulary and arguments appropriate for that audience.	Demonstrates some understanding of the potential reader and uses arguments appropriate for that audience.	It is not clear whom the author is writing for.	
Statement of Claim	The position statement provides a clear, strong statement of the author's position on the topic.	The position statement provides a clear statement of the author's position on the topic.	A position statement is present, but does not make the author's position clear.	There is no position statement.	
Evidence of Examples	All of the evidence and examples are specific and relevant, and explanations are given that show how each piece of evidence supports the author's position.	Most of the evidence and examples are specific and relevant, and explanations are given that show how each piece of evidence supports the author's position.	At least one of the pieces of evidence and examples is relevant and has an explanation that shows how that piece of evidence supports the author's position.	Evidence and examples are NOT relevant AND/OR are not explained.	

Word Choice	All words are well-chosen to convey a clear and consistent tone.	Most words convey a clear tone.	Most words are appropriate, but there is an inconsistent or unclear tone.	Some words are not appropriate for the audience and/or tone.
Sources	All sources used for quotes, ideas, and facts are credible and cited correctly. The author cites at least three readings from class.	All sources used for quotes, ideas, and facts are credible and most are cited correctly. The author cites at least two readings from class.	Most sources used for quotes, ideas, and facts are cited correctly. The author cites at least two readings from class.	Many sources are suspect (not credible) AND/OR are not cited correctly. The author cites fewer than two readings from class.
Grammar & Spelling	Author makes no errors in grammar or spelling that distract the reader from the content.	Author makes one to two errors in grammar or spelling that distract the reader from the content.	Author makes three to four errors in grammar or spelling that distract the reader from the content.	Author makes more than four errors in grammar or spelling that distract the reader from the content.

References

Alexander, B., Adams Becker, S., & Cummins, M. (2016). *Digital literacy: An NMC Horizon Project strategic brief* (Vol. 3.3). Austin, TX: The New Media Consortium.

Alliance for Excellent Education. (2012). The digital learning imperative: How technology and teaching meet today's education challenges. Retrieved from all4ed. org/wp-content/uploads/2012/01/DigitalLearningImperative.pdf

Alotta, R. I. (1990, November). Civil War justice: Union Army executions under Lincoln. Review by Richard Bardolph in *The Journal of Southern History, 56* (4), 762–763. Retrieved from jstor.org.prox.lib.ncsu.edu/stable/2210963

Anderson, L. W., & Krathwohl, D. R. (Eds.). (2001). *A taxonomy for learning, teaching, and assessing: A revision of Bloom's Taxonomy of Educational Objectives.* New York, NY: Longman.

Archer, A. (2011). Exploring the foundations of explicit instruction. In A. Archer & C. Hughes (Eds.), *Explicit instruction: Effective and efficient* (pp. 1–22). New York, NY: Guilford Press.

Asia Society/OECD. (2018). Teaching for global competence in a rapidly changing world. Retrieved from oecd-ilibrary.org/education/teaching-for-global-competence-in-a-rapidly-changing-world_9789264289024-en

Association for Supervision and Curriculum Development (ASCD). (2015). Teacher leadership: The what, why, and how of teachers as leaders. Retrieved from ascd. org/ASCD/pdf/siteASCD/wholechild/fall2014wcsreport.pdf

Beers, K., & Probst, B. (2015). *Reading nonfiction: Notice & note stances, signposts, and strategies.* Portsmouth, NH: Heinemann.

Bezemer, J., & Kress, G. (2008). Writing in multimodal texts: A social semiotic account of designs for learning. *Written Communication, 25*(2), 166–195.

Bishop, R., & Counihan, E. (2018). Beyond the page: New literacies in the twenty-first century. *Voices from the Middle, 25*(4), 39–44.

Boley, T. (1985). New trends in reading comprehension. In *Building successful participant's manual* (pp. 3.2–3.8). New York, NY: The College Board.

Bomer, R., & Bomer, K. (2001). *For a better world: Reading and writing for social action.* Portsmouth, NH: Heinemann.

Brozo, W. G., Moorman, G., Meyer, C., & Steward, T. (2013). Content area reading and disciplinary literacy: A case for the radical center. *Journal of Adolescent & Adult Literacy, 56*(5), 353–357.

Bruner, J. (1960). The act of discovery. *Harvard Educational Review, 31*(1), 21–32.

Buck Institute for Education. (2019). How to get started with PBL. Retrieved from pblworks.org/get-started

Buck Institute for Education. (n.d.). What is PBL? Retrieved from pblworks.org/what-is-pbl

Buehl, D. (2017). *Developing readers in the academic disciplines.* Portland, ME: Stenhouse Publishers.

Cervetti, G. (2014, December). Content area literacy and disciplinary literacy in elementary science: Reconciling the divide. Paper presented at the conference of the Literacy Research Association, Marco Island, FL.

Cervetti, G., & Pearson, P. D. (2012). Reading, writing, and thinking like a scientist. *Journal of Adolescent & Adult Literacy, 55*(7), 580–586. doi:10.1002/JAAL.00069

Chall, J. S. (1996). *Stages of reading development* (2nd ed.). Fort Worth, TX: Harcourt Brace.

Charner-Laird, M., Ippolito, J., & Dobbs, C. L. (2016). The roles of teacher leaders in guiding PLCs focused on disciplinary literacy. *Journal of School Leadership, 26*(6), 975–1001. doi:10.1177/105268461602600604

Cochran-Smith, M., & Lytle, S., (2009). *Inquiry as stance: Practitioner research for the next generation.* New York, NY: Teachers College Press.

Coiro, J. (2003). Reading on the Internet: Expanding our understanding of reading comprehension to encompass new literacies. *The Reading Teacher, 56*(5), 458–464.

Coiro, J. (2011). Predicting reading comprehension on the Internet: Contributions of offline reading skills, online reading skills, and prior knowledge. *Journal of Literacy Research, 43*(4) 352–392.

Coiro, J. (2014, April 7). Teaching adolescents how to evaluate the quality of online information. Retrieved from edutopia.org/blog/evaluating-quality-of-online-info-julie-coiro

College Board. (2004). Pre-AP: Strategies in social studies—Writing tactics using SOAPSTone. Retrieved from secure-media.collegeboard.org/apc/ap04_preap_15_strat_s_36085.pdf

Collins, A., Brown, J. S., & Newman, S. E. (1988). Cognitive apprenticeship: Teaching the craft of reading, writing and mathematics. *Thinking: The Journal of Philosophy for Children, 8*(1), 2–10.

Delpit, L. (2005). *Other people's children: Cultural conflict in the classroom.* New York, NY: New Press.

Dewey, J. (1927). *The public and its problems.* Athens, OH: Shallow.

Dewey, J. (1933). *How we think.* Chicago, IL: Henry Regnery.

Dewey, J. (2004). *Democracy and education.* Mineola, NY: Dover. Original work published 1916.

Dweck, C. (2006). *Mindset—The new psychology of success.* New York, NY: Penguin.

Dwyer, B. (2016). Teaching and learning in the global village: Connect, create, collaborate, and communicate. *The Reading Teacher 70*(1). doi:10.1002/trtr.1500

Ehren, B. J., Murza, K. A., & Malani, M. D. (2012). Disciplinary literacy from a speech-language pathologists' perspective. *Topics in Language Disorders, 32*(1), 85–98.

Factors that Affect the Activity of the Enzyme Catalase. (n.d.). Retrieved from studylib.net/doc/8104820/sample-lab-report--factors-which-affect-the-activity-of-t%20.%20.%20.%20#.XQkMuMCKCx0

Faggella-Luby, M. N., Graner, P. S., Deschler, D. D., & Drew, S. V. (2012). Building a house on sand: Why disciplinary literacy is not sufficient to replace general strategies for adolescent learners who struggle. *Topics in Language Disorders, 32*(1), 69–84.

Fang, Z., & Coatoam, S. (2013). Disciplinary literacy: What you want to know about it. *Journal of Adolescent & Adult Literacy, 56*(8), 627–632.

Fang, Z., & Schleppegrell, M. J. (2010). Disciplinary literacies across content areas: Supporting secondary reading through functional language analysis. *Journal of Adolescent & Adult Literacy, 53*(7), 587–597.

Fisher, D., & Frey, N. (2013). *Better learning through structured teaching: A framework for the gradual release of responsibility* (2nd ed.). Alexandria, VA: ASCD.

Fisher, D., & Frey, N. (2017). Show and tell: A video column/modeling disciplinary thinking. *Educational Leadership: Literacy in Every Classroom, 74*(5), 82–83

Freire, P., & Macedo, D. (1987). *Literacy: Reading the word and the world.* London, England: Routledge.

Frey, N., Fisher, D., & Hernandez, T. (2003). "What's the gist?" Summary writing for struggling adolescent writers. *Voices from the Middle, 11*(2), 43-49.

Galileo Educational Network. (2017). What is inquiry? Retrieved from galileo.org/inquiry-what.html

Gallimore, R., Ermeling, B., Saunders, W., & Goldenberg, C. (2009). Moving the learning of teaching closer to practice: Teacher education implications of school-based inquiry teams. *The Elementary School Journal, 109*(5), 537–553.

Galloway, E. P., Lawrence, J. F., & Moje, E. B. (2013). Research in disciplinary literacy: Challenges and instructional opportunities in teaching disciplinary texts. In J. Ippolito, J. F. Lawrence, & C. Zaller (Eds.), *Adolescent literacy in the era of the Common Core: From research into practice* (pp. 13–36). Cambridge, MA: Harvard Education Press.

Gee, J. P. (2015). *Social linguistics and literacies: Ideology in discourses* (5th ed.). New York, NY: Routledge.

Goldenberg, C. (2008). Teaching English language learners: What the research does—and does not say. *American Educator, 33*(2), 8–44.

Graham, A., Kerkhoff, S., & Spires, H. (2017). Disciplinary literacy in the middle school: Exploring pedagogical tensions. *Middle Grades Research Journal, 11*(1), 63–83.

Hall, L. (2014). *Dr. Leigh Hall discusses disciplinary literacy and struggling readers* [YouTube video]. Retrieved from youtube.com/watch?v=cD4oNr-aIHY

Hansen, D. T. (2008). Curriculum and the idea of a cosmopolitan inheritance. *Journal of Curriculum Studies, 40*(3), 289–312.

Hansen, D. T., Burdick-Shepherd, S., Cammarano, C., & Obelleiro, G. (2009). Education, values, and valuing in cosmopolitan perspective. *Curriculum Inquiry, 39*(5), 587–612.

Hatano, G., & Wertsch, J. V. (2001). Sociocultural approaches to cognitive development: The constituents of culture in the mind. *Human Development, 44*, 77–83.

Hattie, J. (2008). *Visible learning: A synthesis of over 800 meta-analyses relating to achievement.* New York, NY: Routledge.

Hattie, J., & Timperley, H. (2007). The power of feedback. *Review of Educational Research, 77*(1), 81–112.

Hattie, J., & Zierer, K. (2018). *10 mindframes for visible learning: Teaching for success*. New York, NY: Routledge.

Herber, H. L. (1970). *Teaching reading in content areas*. Englewood Cliffs, NJ: Prentice-Hall.

Heritage, M., Walqui, A., & Linquianti, R. (2016). *English language learners and the new standards: Developing language, content knowledge and analytical practices in the classroom*. Cambridge, MA: Harvard Education Press.

Hicks, D., Doolittle, P. E., & Ewing, E. T. (2004). The SCIM-C strategy: Expert historians, historical inquiry, and multimedia. *Social Education, 68*(3), 221–225.

Hillman, A. M. (2014). A literature review on disciplinary literacy: How do secondary teachers apprentice students into mathematical literacy? *Journal of Adolescent & Adult Literacy, 57*(5), 397–406. doi:10.1002/jaal.256

Hinchman, K., & Moore, D. (2013). Close reading: A cautionary interpretation. *Journal of Adolescent and Adult Literacy, 56*(6), 441–450.

Hirsch, C. R., Fey, J. T., Hart, E. W., Schoen, H. L., & Watkins, A. (2008). *Core-plus mathematics: Contemporary mathematics in context*. Columbus, OH: Glencoe/McGraw-Hill.

Homstad, D. W. (2001). Lincoln's agonizing decision. *American History, 36*(5), 28. Retrieved from web.ebscohost.com.prox.lib.ncsu.edu/ehost/detail?sid=088532 25-12e4-4775-84bf-ff7935b9f5fe%40sessionmgr4&vid=3&hid=22&bdata =JnNpdGU9ZWhvc3QtbGl2ZSZzY29wZT1zaXRl#db=ahl&AN=5334427

Hull, G. A., & Stornaiuolo, A. (2010). Literate arts in a global world: Reframing social networking as cosmopolitan practice. *Journal of Adolescent & Adult Literacy 54*(2), 84–96.

Jewitt, C., & Kress, G. (2003). *Multimodal literacy*. New York, NY: Peter Lang.

Johnson, L., Adams Becker, S., Cummins, M., Estrada, V., Freeman, A., & Hall, C. (2016). *NMC Horizon Report: 2016 Higher Education Edition*. Austin, TX: The New Media Consortium.

Kerkhoff, S. (2014, March). *TOADS: A K–12 framework for close reading of complex informational texts*. Paper presented at the North Carolina Research Association Conference, Raleigh, NC.

Kerkhoff, S. (2017). Teaching for global readiness: A model for locally situated and globally connected literacy instruction. In E. Ortlieb & E. Cheek (Eds.), *Addressing diversity in literacy instruction* (pp. 193–205). Bingley, England: Emerald.

Kerkhoff, S., & Spires, H. (2015). Getting close to close reading: Teachers making instructional shifts in early literacy. *Journal of Language and Literacy, 11*(2).

Kingston, S. (2018). Project based learning & student achievement: What does the research tell us? *PBL Evidence Matters, 1*(1), 1–11.

Kress, G. (2003). *Literacy in the new media age*. London, England: Routledge.

Lave, J., & Wenger, E. (1991). *Situated learning: Legitimate peripheral participation*. Cambridge, England: Cambridge University Press.

Learned, J. E. (2018). Doing history: A study of disciplinary literacy and readers labeled as struggling. *Journal of Literacy Research, 50*(2), 190–216.

Lee, C. D., & Spratley, A. (2010). *Reading in the disciplines: The challenges of adolescent literacy*. New York, NY: Carnegie Corporation.

Lee, K. M. (2018). *New approaches to literacies studies in the digital and globalizing world: Border-Crossing Discourses (BCD) in the global online affinity spaces* (Unpublished doctoral dissertation). Arizona State University, Tempe, AZ.

Lent, R. C., & Voigt, M. M., (2019). *Disciplinary literacy in action*. Thousand Oaks, CA: Corwin.

Leu, D. J., Kinzer, C. K., Coiro, J. L., & Cammack, D. W. (2004). Toward a theory of new literacies emerging from the Internet and other information and communication technologies. In R. B. Ruddell & N. J. Unrau (Eds.), *Theoretical models and processes of reading* (5th ed., pp. 1570–1613). Newark, DE: International Reading Association.

Leu, D. J., Kinzer, C. K., Coiro, J., Castek, J., & Henry, L. (2013). New literacies: A dual-level theory of the changing nature of literacy, instruction, and assessment. In D. Alvermann, N. Unrau, & R. Ruddell (Eds.), *Theoretical models and processes of reading* (6th ed., pp. 1150–1181). Newark, DE: International Reading Association.

Lewison, M., Flint, A. S., & Van Sluys, K. (2002). Taking on critical literacy: The journey of newcomers and novices. *Language Arts, 79*, 382–392.

Lewison, M., Leland, C., & Harste, J. (2000). Not in my classroom! The case for using multiview social issues books with children. *The Australian Journal of Language and Literacy, 23*(1), 8–20.

Lieberman, A., & Friedrich, L. (2010). *How teachers become leaders: Learning from practice and research*. New York, NY: Teachers College Press.

Lytle, J., Lytle, S., Johanek, M., & Rho, K. (2018). *Repositioning educational leadership: Practitioners leading from an inquiry stance*. New York, NY: Teachers College Press.

Mayer, R. (2004). Should there be a three-strikes rule against discovery learning? The case for guided methods of instruction. *American Psychologist, 59*(1), 14–19.

McConachie, S. M., & Apodaca, R. E. (2010). Embedding disciplinary literacy leadership and professional learning. In S. M. McConachie & A. R. Petrosky (Eds.), *Content matters: A disciplinary literacy approach to improving student learning* (pp. 163–196). San Francisco, CA: Jossey-Bass. doi:10.1002/9781118269466.ch7

McConachie, S. M., & Petrosky, A. R. (2010). *Content matters: A disciplinary literacy approach to improving student learning*. San Francisco, CA: Jossey-Bass.

McLaughlin, M. (2010). *Content area reading: Teaching and learning in an age of multiple literacies*. New York, NY: Allyn and Bacon.

Mishra, P., & Koehler, M. J. (2006). Technological pedagogical content knowledge: A framework for teacher knowledge. *Teachers College Record, 108*(6), 1017–1054.

Moje, E. B. (2007). Developing socially just subject-matter instruction: A review of the literature on disciplinary literacy. In L. Parker (Ed.), *Review of research in education* (pp. 1–44). Washington, DC: American Educational Research Association.

Moje, E. B. (2015). Doing and teaching disciplinary literacy with adolescent learners: A social and cultural enterprise. *Harvard Educational Review, 85*(2), 254–278.

Moje, E. B., Stockdill, D., Kim, K., & Kim, H. (2011). The role of text in disciplinary learning. In M. Kamil, P. D. Pearson, P. Mosenthal, P. Afflerbach, & E. B. Moje (Eds.), *Handbook of reading research* (Vol. 4, pp. 453–486). Mahwah, NJ: Erlbaum/Taylor & Francis.

National Governors Association Center for Best Practices & Council of Chief State School Officers. (2010). *Common core state standards for English language arts and literacy in history/social studies, science, and technical subjects.* Washington, DC: Authors.

New London Group. (1996). A pedagogy of multiliteracies: Designing social futures. *Harvard Educational Review, 66*(1), 60–92.

Ng, W. (2012). *Empowering scientific literacy through digital literacy and multiliteracies.* New York, NY: Nova Science Publishers.

Nuthall, G. A. (2007). *The hidden lives of learners.* Wellington, New Zealand: New Zealand Council of Educational Research.

O'Brien, D., & Scharber, C. (2008). Digital literacies go to school: Potholes and possibilities. *Journal of Adolescent & Adult Literacy, 52*(1), 66–68.

Organisation for Economic Co-operation and Development. (2018). *Education 2030: The future of education and skills* (Position Paper). Retrieved from oecd.org/education/2030/E2030%20Position%20Paper%20(05.04.2018).pdf

Partnership for Assessment of Readiness for College and Careers. (2011). PARCC model content frameworks: English language arts/literacy grades 3–11 [pdf]. Retrieved from parcconline.org/sites/parcc/files/PARCCMCFELALiteracyAugust2012_Final.pdf

Pearson, P. D., & Gallagher, M. C. (1983). The instruction of reading comprehension. *Contemporary Educational Psychology, 8,* 317–344.

Prüss-Üstün, A., Bos, R., Gore, F., & Bartram, J. (2008). *Safer water, better health: Costs, benefits and sustainability of interventions to protect and promote health.* Geneva, Switzerland: World Health Organization.

Rainey, E., & Moje, E. B. (2012). Building insider knowledge: Teaching students to read, write, and think within ELA and across the disciplines. *English Education, 45*(1), 71–90.

ReadWriteThink/IRA/NCTE. (2011). TP-CASTT poetry analysis. Retrieved from readwritethink.org/files/resources/30738_analysis.pdf

Ripp, P. (2017). *Reimagining literacy through global collaboration.* Bloomington, IN: Solution Tree Press.

Ritchhart, R. (2015). *Creating cultures of thinking: The 8 forces we must master to truly transform our schools.* San Francisco, CA: John Wiley & Sons.

Rosenblatt, L. (1978). *The reader, the text, the poem: The transactional theory of reading and writing.* Carbondale, IL: Southern Illinois University Press.

Schoenbach, R., Greenleaf, C., & Murphy, L. (2012). *Reading for understanding: How reading apprenticeship improves disciplinary learning in secondary and college classrooms.* New York, NY: John Wiley & Sons.

Shanahan, C., Shanahan, T., & Misischia, C. (2011). Analysis of expert readers in three disciplines: History, mathematics, and chemistry. *Journal of Literacy Research, 43*(4), 393–429.

Shanahan, T., Fisher, D., & Frey, N. (2012). The challenge of challenging text. *Educational Leadership, 69*(6), 58–63.

Shanahan, T., & Shanahan, C. (2008). Teaching disciplinary literacy to adolescents: Rethinking content-area literacy. *Harvard Educational Review, 78*(1), 40–59.

Short, K. G. (2009). Inquiry as a stance on curriculum. In S. Davidson & S. Carber (Eds.), *Taking the PYP forward* (pp. 11–26). Woodbridge, England: John Catt Educational.

Shulman, L. S. (1986). Those who understand: Knowledge growth in teaching. *Educational Researcher, 15*(2), 4–14.

Skerrett, A., Warrington, A., & Williamson, T. (2018). Generative principles for professional learning for equity-oriented urban English teachers. *English Education, 50*(2), 116–146.

Snow, C. (2002). *Reading for understanding: Toward an R&D program in reading comprehension.* Santa Monica, CA: RAND Corporation.

Spires, H. A., Hervey, L., Morris, G., & Stelpflug, C. (2012). Energizing project-based inquiry: Middle grade students read, write, and create videos. *Journal of Adolescent & Adult Literacy, 55*(6), 483–493.

Spires, H. A., Himes, M. P., Medlock Paul, C., & Kerkhoff, S. N. (2019). Going global with project-based inquiry: Cosmopolitan literacies in practice. *Journal of Adolescent & Adult Literacy.* doi:10.1002/jaal.947

Spires, H. A., Kerkhoff, S., & Fortune, N. (2018). Educational cosmopolitanism and collaborative inquiry with Chinese and U.S. teachers. *Teaching Education.* doi: 10.1080/10476210.2018.1506431

Spires, H. A., Kerkhoff, S. N., & Graham, A. C. K. (2016). Disciplinary literacy and inquiry: Teaching for deeper learning. *Journal of Adolescent and Adult Literacy, 60*(2), 51–61.

Spires, H. A., Kerkhoff, S. N., Graham, A. C. K., & Lee, J. K. (2014). *Relating inquiry to disciplinary literacy: A pedagogical approach.* Raleigh, NC: Friday Institute of Educational Innovation, North Carolina State University.

Spires, H. A., Kerkhoff, S. N., Graham, A. C. K., Thompson, I., & Lee, J. K. (2018). Operationalizing and validating disciplinary literacy in secondary education. *Reading and Writing, 31*(6), 1401–1434.

Spires, H. A., Medlock Paul, C., Himes, H., & Yuan, C. (2018). Cross-cultural collaborative inquiry: A collective case study with students from China and the U.S. *International Journal of Educational Research, 91*, 28–40.

Spires, H. A., Wiebe, E., Young, C., Hollebrands, K., & Lee, J. (2009). Toward a new learning ecology: Teaching and learning in 1:1 learning environments. *Friday Institute White Paper Series.* Raleigh, NC: North Carolina State University.

Street, B. (2003). What's "new" in New Literacy Studies? Critical approaches to literacy in theory and practice. *Current Issues in Comparative Education, 5*(2), 77–91.

Sweller, J. (1988). Cognitive load during problem solving: Effects on learning. *Cognitive Science, 12*(2), 257–285.

Thomas, S., Joseph, C., Laccetti, J., Mason, B., Mills, S., Perril, S., & Pullinger, K. (2007). Transliteracy: Crossing divides. *FirstMonday, 12*(12). doi:10.5210/fm.v12i12.2060

Thompson, H. (n.d.). Exchange of prisoners in the Civil War. *The Photographic History of The Civil War, 4.* Retrieved from civilwarhome.com/prisonerexchange.htm

Tomlinson, C. A. (2017). *How to differentiate instruction* (3rd ed.). Alexandria, VA: ASCD.

Tomlinson, C. A., & McTighe, J. (2006). *Integrating differentiated instruction: Understanding by design.* Alexandria, VA: ASCD.

United Nations. (n.d.). About the sustainable development goals. Retrieved from un.org/sustainabledevelopment/sustainable-development-goals/

Vilson, J. (2013, August 7). What teacher leadership looks like for the new school year. Retrieved from edutopia.org/blog/teacher-leadership-new-school-year-jose-vilson

Vygotsky, L. (1978). *Mind in society: The development of higher psychological processes.* Cambridge, MA: Harvard University Press.

Wahlström, N. (2014). Toward a conceptual framework for understanding cosmopolitanism on the ground. *Curriculum Inquiry, 44*(1), 113–132.

Walqui, A., & Lier, L. (2010). *Scaffolding the academic success of adolescent English language learners: A pedagogy of promise.* San Francisco, CA: WestEd.

WHO/UNICEF. (2006). Meeting the MDG drinking-water and sanitation target. Retrieved from who.int/water_sanitation_health/monitoring/jmp2006/en

Wiggins, G. (1998). *Educative assessment: Designing assessments to inform and improve student performance.* San Francisco, CA: Jossey-Bass.

Wilder, P., & Msseemmaa, D. (2019). Centering disciplinary literacies on student consciousness: A Tanzanian case study. *Journal of Adolescent & Adult Literacy, 62*(5), 479–484.

Wilhelm, J. (2007). *Engaging readers and writers with inquiry: Promoting understandings in language arts and the content areas with guiding questions.* New York, NY: Scholastic.

Wineburg, S. S. (1991). On the reading of historical texts: Notes on the breach between school and academy. *American Educational Research Journal, 28*(3), 495–519. doi:10.3102/00028312028003495

Wittenberg, E. J. (2012). Lives on the line. *Civil War Times, 51*(4), 58–65. Retrieved from web.ebscohost.com.prox.lib.ncsu.edu/ehost/detail?sid=08853225-12e4-4775-84bf-ff7935b9f5fe%40sessionmgr4&vid=6&hid=22&bdata=JnNpdGU9ZWhvc3QtbGl2ZSZzY29wZT1zaXRl#db=a9h&AN=7634097

Wood, D., Bruner, J., & Ross, G. (1976). The role of tutoring in problem solving. *The Journal of Child Psychology and Psychiatry, 17*, 89–100.

Yoon, B., Yol, Ö., Haag, C., & Simpson, A. (2018). Critical global literacies: A new instructional framework in the global era. *Journal of Adolescent & Adult Literacy, 62*(2), 205–214.

York-Barr, J., & Duke, K. (2004). What do we know about teacher leadership? Findings from two decades of scholarship. *Review of Educational Research, 74*(3), 255–316.

Zygouris-Coe, V. I. (2012). Disciplinary literacy and the Common Core State Standards. *Topics in Language Disorders, 32*(1), 35–50.

Index

About the Authors

Hiller A. Spires is an alumni-distinguished graduate professor at the College of Education and senior research fellow at the Friday Institute for Educational Innovation at North Carolina State University. She directs the New Literacies & Global Learning master's program and the New Literacies Collaborative at NC State. Her research focuses on the integration of emerging technologies in order to illustrate research-based best practices for digital and disciplinary literacy learning with diverse populations. She also studies teacher and student inquiry processes during collaboration on compelling issues across time, space, and culture. She has authored over 200 peer-reviewed articles and scholarly papers. Dr. Spires was the founding director of the Friday Institute for Educational Innovation from 2002–2006 and recently helped create a state-of-the-art high school in Suzhou, China.

Shea N. Kerkhoff is an assistant professor of secondary education at the University of Missouri–St. Louis. She holds a Ph.D. from North Carolina State University in Literacy and English Language Arts. She taught high school English for seven years, including North Carolina and District of Columbia public schools, and currently serves as assistant editor of *English Education*, a National Council of Teachers of English journal. She also serves as Going Global, Inc.'s Education Director. Dr. Kerkhoff is passionate about literacy education at home and abroad. In 2018 she was named a Longview Foundation Global Teacher Educator fellow. Her work focuses on critical, digital, and global literacies; disciplinary literacy; and teacher education. Uniting these three foci is an inquiry stance for teaching and learning.

Casey Medlock Paul is an adult and online learning specialist at the Justice Research and Statistics Association. She earned her Ph.D. in Literacy and English Language Arts from the College of Education at North Carolina State University and received the first-place award for outstanding dissertation at the Graduate Student Research Symposium in 2018. Her research focuses on critical literacy pedagogy, disciplinary literacy, and English Language Learners. Before receiving her Ph.D., Dr. Paul taught high school Spanish in Alabama.